CU00926165

The Observer's Pocket Series

GOLF

The Observer Books

A POCKET REFERENCE SERIES
COVERING A WIDE RANGE OF SUBJECTS

Natural History
BIRDS
BIRDS' EGGS
BUTTERFLIES
LARGER MOTHS
COMMON INSECTS
WILD ANIMALS
ZOO ANIMALS
WILD FLOWERS
GARDEN FLOWERS
FLOWERING TREES
  AND SHRUBS
HOUSE PLANTS
CACTI
TREES
GRASSES
COMMON FUNGI
LICHENS
POND LIFE
FRESHWATER FISHES
SEA FISHES
SEA AND SEASHORE
GEOLOGY
ASTRONOMY
WEATHER
CATS
DOGS
HORSES AND PONIES

Sport
ASSOCIATION FOOTBALL
CRICKET
GOLF
MOTOR SPORT

Transport
AIRCRAFT
AUTOMOBILES
COMMERCIAL VEHICLES
SHIPS
MANNED SPACEFLIGHT
UNMANNED
  SPACEFLIGHT
BRITISH STEAM
  LOCOMOTIVES

The Arts, etc.
ARCHITECTURE
CATHEDRALS
CHURCHES
HERALDRY
FLAGS
PAINTING
MODERN ART
SCULPTURE
FURNITURE
MUSIC
POSTAGE STAMPS
POTTERY AND
  PORCELAIN
BRITISH AWARDS
  AND MEDALS
EUROPEAN COSTUME
SEWING

Cities
LONDON

The Observer's Book of

GOLF

TOM SCOTT

WITH 8 COLOUR PLATES
AND 26 BLACK-AND-WHITE
PHOTOGRAPHS

FREDERICK WARNE

LONDON

Published by
Frederick Warne (Publishers) Ltd
London

© Frederick Warne & Co Ltd 1975
Reprinted 1977

Library of Congress Catalog
Card No 73–80250

ISBN 0 7232 1520 0

Printed in Great Britain at
The Pitman Press, Bath
1640.377

CONTENTS

LIST OF COLOUR PLATES

FOREWORD

Golf is played in practically every country in the world except Russia and China. And with the breaking down of international barriers these countries, which are now making such enormous strides in other sports, could soon be taking up the game with the same enthusiasm that they have embraced gymnastics, football, table tennis, badminton and other sports.

Golf's army, already many millions strong, is growing daily. Players fall into many categories, from the star professionals and highly skilled amateurs down to humble club men and women, playing perhaps just once a week, and those who manage the odd game on a public course.

Without exception, they all want to improve. That applies as much to the professionals striving for the big cash awards that success now brings, as it does to the lesser accomplished.

Whatever the ambition or the standard, every player should know the common golfing terms and the courtesies expected on the course.

It adds to the enjoyment, too, to know about the game's great figures, past and present, the famous clubs, winners of championships and countless other interesting facts accumulated through the ages.

This illustrated book is, as far as I am aware, the first pocket-sized volume of its kind. It sets out to be not only a source of information but of pleasure to all who are interested in it.

For easy reference the main section has been arranged in a comprehensive A to Z pattern which gives golf terms and numerous other facts.

Throughout the book there are cross-references to help the reader follow up any particular line of interest as easily and quickly as possible.

Preparation has necessitated considerable research and I have been fortunate in having the advice and help of two famous British golf correspondents, now retired.

They are Mr Geoffrey Cousins, formerly of the London *Star* and *Daily Telegraph,* and Mr Maurice Hart, formerly of the London *Evening News.* I trust our long-standing friendships have not been too sorely tried as a result of my constant approaches to them.

On a few occasions, too, I have had recourse to that golfers' bible *The Golfers' Handbook* of which another old friend Mr Percy Huggins is editor. To him, also, I give grateful thanks.

I like to believe that the end result will give pleasure to everyone for whom golf means something.

TOM SCOTT

Chalfont St Giles
January 1975

PHOTOGRAPH ACKNOWLEDGEMENTS

Thanks are given to the following for their kind permission to reproduce photographs used in this book: Action Photos (H. W. Neale) for photos on Pls 1, 2, 5 (above), 7 and 8, and on pages 35 (below right), 74 (below), 115 and 137 (above); Essex Sport Picture Services (Mike Street) for photos on Pl 5 (below); Associated Press Ltd for page 137 (below); S. H. Benson for Pl 4 (above) and page 51; Central Press photos for pages 73 and 116 (left); Peter Dazeley for page 35 (below left); *The Field* for page 53; Irish Touring for page 52 (below); E. D. Lacey for pages 75, 116 (right) and 117 (right); J. D. MacDonald for page 33 (below); Jack Nowland for Pl 6; Press Association for page 117 (left); Special Press for page 33 (above); Syndication International for Pl 3; and Topical Press Agency for pages 34 (below) and 136. While every effort has been made to trace copyright owners of photographs, the publishers apologize for any oversights which might have occurred.

HISTORY OF GOLF

Man has long hit one object with another as a form of recreation, though perhaps at first it was not more than hitting a rock with some rough-hewn article.

The Romans had a game called *paganica* which American golf historian, Mr Charles Price, described as one played with a bent stick and a ball stuffed with feathers. Presumably there were rules, or it could have been that the object was merely to hit the ball as far as possible. In fact it sounded more like hockey than anything else.

The Roman legions spread far and wide, and so it is not surprising that games similar to *paganica* were played in parts of Europe such as France, Holland and Belgium. This fact is invariably quoted by those who support the theory that golf was first played in the Low Countries, the Netherlands of today. I have seen a map which Mr van Hengel, a distinguished Dutch golfer, maintains is one of a golf course around the year 1400. If Mr van Hengel is correct then it proves that golf was played in his country before there was any mention of it in Scotland.

But what supporters of the Netherlands theory forget is that a game sometimes referred to as club-ball and Cambuca (also played with a club and a ball) was in Britain as early as 1363. We know this because an edict issued by the Sheriff of Kent banned it that year.

Hockey in England goes back much further. Also in 1363 a boy of ten was imprisoned for being responsible for the death of another boy at Lincoln, the cause being a blow on the head while playing hockey.

While such games were certainly being played in England, there is little in writing concerning them and no drawings of any kind showing the participants in action.

Not so in the Netherlands where famous artists started to paint pictures of ball games known by various names such as *kolf, kolven,* and *chole.* A beautiful book of 183 vellum pages, the *Book of the Hours,* executed by Simon Bening of Bruges in 1530, shows pictures of figures playing a game with a club and a ball. The club appears as a crude early golf club or hockey stick and the ball, a wooden one, resembles a hockey ball. Many fine paintings appear in art galleries in Holland depicting people playing ball games.

Because the early Dutch games were so profusely illustrated around the 16th century it has always been accepted by many that these pictures prove that golf started in Holland. But similar games were being played in other parts of Europe, particularly France, which had *Le Jeu de Mail* which later became Pell Mell or Pall Mall.

This, like most of the other games except *kolven,* was played without boundaries, and it is suggested that London's famous streets, Pall Mall and The Mall, or the land on which they now stand, were once used for Pell Mell which had found its way from France.

Apart from Mr van Hengel's map there is no evidence to prove that any of the early games being played were golf. Yet it does show that the Dutch were trying to compromise between one of their games which had no boundaries and another played in an enclosed space.

Many historians seem to have become confused by the evidence of the early Dutch pictures and forgotten that golf was played in Scotland long before any of the Dutch paintings of ball games were executed. For instance, the *Book of the Hours* appeared in 1530 and the first mention of 'golfe' or golf in Scotland was in 1457 when the Scottish Parliament banned the game because it interfered with the archery practice of the citizens. The Act of Parliament would not have been brought if the game had not grown to such an extent as to make the edict necessary. The penalty for violation was a fine but there is no record of anyone being convicted. The Scottish people persisted in playing golf, but it was not until 1618 that official permission for it was granted by the king, although the Act had been made obsolete a few years earlier by the invention of gunpowder which superseded the bow as the principal weapon of warfare.

A decree some 30 years earlier made no specific mention of golf so it can be concluded that it became popular in the period between the decrees. It may well have started long before the first but made only slow progress.

Trading went on between the Scots and the Low Countries and I support the idea that the Scots merchants saw ball games played on the Continent, brought them home, and then adapted them to suit their own purpose. This is a much more likely theory than that the Scots came to England, saw ball games played, and took them north across the border. Relations between the two countries in those days were hardly conducive to peaceful pastimes.

Some support the theory that Scottish soldiers of fortune may have brought back ideas for ball games from those that they had seen played abroad. These fighting men eventually became the Royal Scots Regiment, the 1st of Foot and the oldest infantry regiment in the British army, who fought campaigns in many lands.

There is no doubt that the Scots were assisted in the transition from ball games to golf by the natural landscape of the countryside, having around their shores many tracts from which the sea had receded, leaving large areas of sandhills interspersed with beautiful clean turf. Such land was public property so it was natural that golfers should gravitate there. One such area of land was at Leith, now part of Scotland's capital, Edinburgh, where golf was first played.

St Andrews and the Royal and Ancient Club which became the headquarters of the ruling body of the game and the greatest golf centre in the world, was not used until 1500 or perhaps a little later. Before then, the game was being played at Perth, some 50 miles (80 km) from Edinburgh. Perth had a royal palace and James IV, a grandson of James II who issued the 1457 decree, became a golf addict. It is on record that he paid 14 Scots shillings, worth one-twelfth of an English shilling (though the English shilling had not yet come into existence at this time), to a bow-maker in Perth for the supply of golf clubs, indicating that bow-makers were in fact the first makers of golf clubs.

It is also on record that the king's treasurer was continually paying money for his master's golf debts and for golf equipment.

For a time at any rate, the king's interest lay elsewhere, for he made a political marriage with Margaret, the daughter of Henry VII of England. However, it would appear that James still retained his liking for golf and actually succeeded in interesting some members of the English Court in the game. In fact, there are grounds for believing that some of Henry's subjects also played.

Peace between England and Scotland was only temporary and when the countries warred once more James lost his life at the battle of Flodden.

With his death it appears that the English promptly lost interest in the game, although it might well have been played around London. Yet in Scotland the game flourished, for the next king, James V, was a keen player and he passed on his liking for the game to his daughter, the ill-fated Mary, Queen of Scots, who played with some enthusiasm.

After the union of the crowns it was left to Mary's son, James VI of Scotland and I of England, to take golf to England on a more permanent basis. Perhaps he was the most enthusiastic of all the royal golfers and when he succeeded to the throne of England and took up residence there he obviously brought his clubs with him and began playing near his palace at Greenwich. It was not unnatural, therefore, that the first golf club in England, the Royal Blackheath, should be established in the district. The actual foundation date of this famous club is in doubt. As the king played immediately he came to England there is a legend that the Society of Golfers at Blackheath was formed in 1608. It is probable that the king and his followers did play at Blackheath, as well as nearby Greenwich, but there is no written evidence that the club dates back to 1608.

The generally accepted date of the club's formation is 1766, but I feel that it is being unduly modest and that it came into being more than 20 years before then.

The formation of the Royal Blackheath Club was a landmark in the game, certainly in England, for it was partly due to the enthusiasm of their members that England's first club with a seaside links was formed. This was the North Devon and Westward Ho! but much later, in 1864.

The game had long been spreading in Scotland and in 1744 those who played on Leith Links formed themselves into a golfing society. This was named the Company of Edinburgh Golfers and was the forerunner of the famous Honourable Company of Edinburgh Golfers who left the little five-hole course for Musselburgh and later for their present home at Muirfield, the venue of many championships. Its first trophy was a silver club presented by the Lord Provost, magistrates and Council of the City of Edinburgh. In 1764 conditions of membership of the society were imposed, and so the first golf club was formed.

This claim is disputed by the Royal Burgess Society of Edinburgh. Certainly there was a collective body of golfers other than the Company of Edinburgh Golfers in existence probably around 1735—and that body it is claimed later became the

Royal Burgess. But many plump for the Company of Edinburgh Golfers as being the oldest club because of its conditions of membership of 1764.

No doubt exists about the date of birth of the Royal Musselburgh Club, which was in 1774. During the 18th century many other Scots clubs were founded and the game was played throughout the country.

The Society of St Andrews Golfers came into being on the 14th May 1754, when 'twenty-two Noblemen and Gentlemen, being admirers of the ancient and healthful exercise of golf' met and drew up certain rules under which they wished to play. The rules were based on those drawn up by the Company of Edinburgh Golfers ten years previously and were admirably clear and brief:

I. You must tee the ball within a club's length of the hole. (This will refer to the hole just played from a stated point.)

II. You must tee the ball on the ground.

III. You are not to change the ball you strike off the tee.

IV. You are not to remove stones, bones or any breakclub for the sake of playing your ball except upon the fair green, and that only within a club's length of your ball.

V. If your ball come among water, or any watery filth, you are at liberty to take out your ball and bringing it behind the hazard, and teeing it, you may play it with any club allowing your adversary a stroke for so getting out your ball.

VI. If your balls be found anywhere touching one another, you are to lift the first ball, till you play the last.

VII. At holing you are to play the ball honestly for the hole, and not to play on your adversary's ball, not lying on your way to the hole.

VIII. If you should lose your ball by its being taken up, or any other way, you are to go back to the spot where you struck last and drop another ball and allow your adversary a stroke for the misfortune.

IX. No man at holing his ball is to be allowed to mark his way to the hole with his clubs or anything else.

X. If a ball be stop'd by any person, horse, dog or anything else the ball so stop'd must be played where it lyes.

XI. If you draw your club in order to strike, and proceed so far in the stroke as to be bringing down your club—if then your club shall break in any way, it is to be accounted a stroke.

XII. He whose ball lyes farthest from the hole is obliged to play first.

XIII. Neither trench, ditch nor dyke made for the preservation of the links, nor the scholars' holes, or the soldiers' lines, shall be accounted a hazard, but the ball is to be taken out, teed and played with any iron club. [Scholars' holes referred to a piece of land on which children played and in doing so made holes. Soldiers' lines is not so clear, but could refer to some entrenchments or earthworks made by soldiers in training.]

These then are the oldest rules of the game. For many years each society or club made its own rules but gradually the set of rules drawn up by the St Andrews Club (it became the Royal and Ancient Club in 1834) came to be universally adopted, though not until 1897, twelve years after the Wimbledon Club had suggested a general set. Today there are forty-one rules with many sub-sections, as opposed to the thirteen original rules which in principal still apply.

Since many golfers played under the St Andrews rules, it was not surprising that the Royal and Ancient Club of St Andrews became the ruling body of the game. It had been more or less accepted as such for many years.

The Royal and Ancient Club seems to have had greatness thrust upon it rather than deliberately seeking success, for three of the great landmarks of the game, certainly as far as Britain is concerned, were reached without much encouragement from the club.

The Amateur Championship was begun through the enterprise of some far-sighted members of the Royal Liverpool at Hoylake, the Open Championship was initiated by the Prestwick Club and the general set of rules idea emanated from the Royal Wimbledon Club in London. Members at Wimbledon were also responsible for the inception of the British Ladies' Championship.

If slow to take on the role of pioneers, it is only fair to say that the Royal and Ancient Club was quick to lend support to such events as the Amateur and the Open Championships, along with others such as the British Boys' Championship which come under their jurisdiction.

Undoubtedly the first British Open Championship at Prestwick in 1860 gave a fillip to the game in Scotland. True, there was only a handful of competitors, but the fact that it was held at all proved that the game was important enough for men to make their living from it, the early professionals being either green-keepers or caddies.

For some years before 1860 some of these professionals were backed by wealthy supporters in matches against each other. The men of St Andrews and Musselburgh, then the two great golfing centres in Scotland, were often in action.

St Andrews had Allan Robertson, the two Morrises (Old Tom and Young Tommy), the Straths, Bob Martin, Tom Kidd and Jamie Anderson, and later the Kirkaldys and Willie Auchterlonie. Musselburgh had the Dunns, the Parks, Bob Ferguson and Dave Brown.

The stakes were considerable and it is said that Robertson and Young Tommy Morris once played the Dunns for £400, which was a fortune in those days. In 1843 Robertson beat Willie Dunn in a marathon 360-hole match.

Robertson was one of the most famous manufacturers of the feather ball in the days when enough feathers to fill a tall hat were stuffed into a leather cover. Old Tom Morris was one of his assistants but the two parted company when Tom became converted to the guttie ball (made of gutta-percha). Robertson also had another claim to fame for he introduced iron clubs.

Morris, who became green-keeper at Prestwick and later returned to his native St Andrews, was four times Open champion, a feat equalled by his son, Tommy, before his early death at 24.

Such, then, were the first professionals who did much to publicize and popularize the game until its great era at the end of the last century when 'the great triumvirate'—Braid, Taylor and Vardon, began to make golf the popular spectacle it has now become.

At about the same time the first Amateur Championship was played, at Hoylake in 1885. The amateurs had in their ranks some talented golfers such as Harold Hilton and John Ball who both won the British Open Championship. Hilton's feat was perhaps the more meritorious because his win in 1897 came when the Triumvirate had appeared.

Women golfers were not to be outdone and the British Ladies' Championship was introduced in 1893, mainly due to the hard work and enthusiasm of Miss Isette Pearson, who was also responsible for the founding of the Ladies' Golf Union.

Of many fine women golfers none was greater than Miss Joyce Wethered, later Lady Heathcoat Amory, who many claimed was as good as the leading male amateurs of her time. It was a pity her serious career ended before the great American, the late Mrs George Zaharias, came on the scene.

Mrs Zaharias who had been an Olympic Gold Medal athlete

was, as Miss Wethered had been, the outstanding woman golfer of her age.

France with a small golfing public has produced some fine women players, providing a mother and daughter who both won the British Championship. They were Mlle Simone de la Chaume (later Madame Lacoste, wife of the famous tennis player) and her daughter Catherine. The mother won in 1927, the daughter in 1969.

The success of French women golfers is proof that if the game spread slowly in that country its foundations were soundly laid.

Naturally enough the Scots took the game to France just as a Scot was responsible for the birth of golf in the United States.

The club at Pau in the Basque region of France is the oldest club in Europe outside Britain. It was founded in 1856 by the Duke of Hamilton and other British enthusiasts who wintered there.

Yet again there is a tradition that British officers first played golf in France, the story being that one or two army men billeted at Pau during the Peninsular War engaged in the game. This is possible but, if true, their golf would have been limited to knocking golf balls about on some spare piece of land.

France has produced few outstanding professionals, but in 1907 a stocky Basque, Arnaud Massy, won the British Open Championship at a time when Braid, Taylor and Vardon were at their peak.

Unfortunately golf in France remains the prerogative of the wealthy and the number of courses is comparatively few. But there are signs that the game is spreading faster now than it has done previously. That being so, the quantity and quality of its players will become evident.

The Scots also took golf to India, which for many years has had trading connections, particularly in jute. Many of them came from Dundee, halfway between the two great golfing centres, Carnoustie and St Andrews.

The Royal Calcutta Club came into being in 1829 to become the oldest golf club outside Scotland or England and was followed by the Royal Bombay Club in 1842. India can also claim the oldest national championship outside the British Isles. It was first played in 1892.

Canada can boast an old golf club in the Royal Montreal which was formed in 1873 just two years before the Royal

Quebec. But, as in France, there is a tradition that golf was played in Canada long before the formation of the first club and that a Glasgow sailor, William Dibmann, amused himself when away from his ship by playing on the famous Heights of Abraham.

Scottish soldiers are also reported to have played there, so it is possible that Canada had golf before the United States.

Canada has a fine tradition of golf despite their winter climate curtailing play. Scots emigrated there to teach the game, and in the early days especially laid strong foundations just as did the many hundreds of Scottish golf professionals in the United States.

As well as going east and west the Scots, with the English, spread further south to Australia and New Zealand. In 1870 the Royal Adelaide Club was formed and the oldest New Zealand club, the Royal Christchurch, followed three years later.

Golf in both countries flourishes and there have been successful professionals from them, such as Peter Thomson who has won the British Open Championship five times, Kel Nagle and Bob Charles, both of whom have a British Open Championship to their credit. Nagle won the Centenary Open at St Andrews in 1960. Australia now has younger golfers such as Crampton, Newton and Devlin who have become leading tournament players.

Golf did not reach South Africa as early as it did in Australia and New Zealand, and the oldest clubs in the Republic, the Royal Cape and the Maritzberg Club, did not come into being until 1885. There is some debate as to which is the oldest as both were founded about the same time, but perhaps the Royal Cape has the edge.

Just before World War II a slender young South African amateur Arthur D'Arcy Locke, was hailed as a golf prodigy. His promise was held in check by the war in which he served in the South African forces, but afterwards he became a professional and won four British Open Championships, in 1949, 1950, 1952 and 1957, as well as scoring many other successes, some of them in the United States. Locke had a very individual style but in the art of putting he has had no peer.

His exploits spurred other young South Africans and Gary Player has proved a worthy successor. Like Locke, he has had many successes including the winning of three British Open Championships.

But if Player's successes in Britain's greatest golfing event have not been as numerous as that of Locke, certainly in the United States he has had more victories, for in that country he has won the Open Championship, the Masters Tournament and the P.G.A. Championship.

Player, too, has inspired other South Africans and the best of the youngest crop are Dale Hayes and Bobby Cole, the latter having won the British Amateur Championship at Carnoustie in 1966.

There is also much interest in golf in the Far East where the Royal Hong Kong Club was established in 1889. Golf was at one time played in China at Shanghai, as indeed it was in Russia which had two courses, one in Moscow and one in St Petersburg as Leningrad was formerly called. Both these courses were mostly used by foreign diplomats, as is now the case with the Bucharest Golf Club in Rumania.

Japan, however, is now enjoying the biggest boom. Golf was taken to that country many years ago by a British businessman, but made no considerable progress until comparatively recently. Now to play golf in Japan is the 'done' thing.

The only hindrance to much faster progress is the lack of land, but the Japanese have countered that with characteristic thoroughness by establishing many driving ranges, where players can hire balls and bang away to their heart's content.

Of the larger countries, only Russia and China stand aloof from the game, but the Russians have lately taken to tennis, so golf might well be the next sport to attract them.

Golf is played in some unlikely places, such as the island of St Helena whose first golf club was formed in 1903. Iceland has several courses and one exists inside the Arctic Circle in Norway.

The United States still leads as the No. 1 golfing country with its thousands of courses and millions of players. In Britain the game is booming, and on the mainland of Europe new courses are regularly coming into use, particularly in Spain. The result is that the quality of play is improving fast in that country and Spanish professionals have proved their worth in recent years. The same applies to their Spanish-speaking cousins in South America from where have come such famous golfers as Roberto de Vicenzo who won the British Open Championship in 1967.

The eight humble men who went to Prestwick to compete in the first British Open Championship could never have dreamed that a hundred years later the event would be one of the world's great sporting spectacles.

And the game has nowhere reached its peak. Its continuing growth will only be limited in some countries such as Britain through lack of land to build courses.

The game will continue to give enormous pleasure to untold millions who have never played it. Attendances at major events such as the United States Open and the British Open prove that. Millions more watch on television, which provides viewers with the opportunity of seeing the world's stars in action in various challenge matches, often at close quarters. Such programmes have done much to popularize the game.

History of American Golf

If there is some dispute whether golf actually began in Scotland, there is no argument as to who spread the game throughout the world. Lack of employment coupled with their pioneering instincts prompted the Scots to emigrate in their thousands during the last century. Many crossed the Atlantic, so it is not surprising that before long they took golf with them just as some took it south into England and then elsewhere.

The game was introduced to the United States by Scottish officers during the American War of Independence. But after their departure golf languished until a club came into being at Savannah. Neither that nor a club at Charleston seem to have lasted long, however, and the game appears to have lapsed until 1884 when the Oakhurst Club was formed at White Sulphur Springs. That club lasted ten years to be followed by the Greenbrier Club.

Doubtless golfers in Charleston and Savannah will claim that their districts saw the birth of the game in America, but since these clubs had only a short tenure of life they are generally discounted in the records.

It is universally conceded that the undisputed golf pioneer in the United States was Mr John Reid, a native of Scotland, who with his friends formed the St Andrews Club at Yonkers, New York, in 1888. Their first course consisted of three holes, and it was laid out in a field owned by Reid. Reid knew something about golf and after he had become successful in his new country he decided he would like to play again.

His friend, Robert Lockhart, was visiting his native Scotland and Reid commissioned him to purchase some clubs and balls, which he did from Tom Morris at St Andrews. The request was for six clubs and two dozen balls. But the men of St Andrews could not fulfil the humble order in time for Lockhart to take the clubs back with him so they had to be shipped by sea.

Six clubs and two dozen balls were not enough to satisfy the growing demands of the golfers in America so more supplies were ordered. The pioneers, among them Henry O. Tallmadge, later to become the first secretary of the Amateur Golf Association of America (now the United States Golf Association), moved to another piece of land owned by a German butcher, named Shotts or Shultz. A six-hole course was laid out and it was then that the St Andrews Club was formed.

But in 1892 the land was required for building so the enthusiasts moved again, just along the road to an apple orchard, and this location gave the pioneers the name of the 'Apple Tree Gang'.

So keen were others to join the club that another move became necessary to a nine-hole course. But even three extra holes were not enough to cope with the rush of new golfers, so three years later they had to find a fourth site, this time an eighteen-hole course at Mount Hope, in Westchester County, New York, where the club has remained to this day.

It was only a matter of time before other clubs came into being and new enthusiasts appeared, including Theodore A. Havemeyer, who after seeing golf being played at Pau in France started a club at Newport, Rhode Island. Mr Havemeyer became the first President of the national association when it was formed in 1894. The founder clubs were St Andrews, the Country Club of Brookline, Newport, Shinnecock Hills and Chicago.

The fact that the game had been taken to Chicago and that a club had been established there shows just how quickly interest in golf was growing, and linked with Chicago was one of the most remarkable of the early American golfers, Charles Blair Macdonald.

He was born in New York but was sent to St Andrews in Scotland to be educated, perhaps, as his name suggests, because he had Scottish antecedents. At St Andrews he played with Tom Morris and other great men of the day.

When he returned to Chicago, he could find no kindred spirit,

20

and the only golf he played during the next few years was on business trips to Britain. But in 1892 several Englishmen went to Chicago in connection with the World Fair and they began interesting some young men in playing the game.

Macdonald, given the task of laying out a course, persuaded some friends at a Chicago social club to have one made under his supervision. Later he constructed a far more ambitious course at Wheaton, a few miles from Chicago.

So if John Reid was the 'father' of American golf, Macdonald was certainly the 'father' of Chicago golf. And he made his influence felt in yet another way: as a result of his constant bickering with others, the great early pioneers, Theodore Havemeyer, Laurence Curtis and Henry Tallmadge, were prompted to set up some recognized body to settle disputes and to make laws. Thus, in 1894, the Amateur Golf Association of the United States was formed. Later, when the association became connected with professional golf, its name was changed to the American Golf Association, and, subsequently, to its present name, The United States Golf Association.

The strange thing is that John Reid was not one of the first office-bearers of the new body. Havemeyer was the first president, Tallmadge the first secretary. It has been suggested that Havemeyer who was a wealthy man was given the top office because of his money and influence. But the fact remains he was a good choice.

Macdonald became second vice-president which no doubt pacified him to some extent although by all accounts he was a difficult man and not easily placated. However, being a born rebel and fond of speaking his mind, he was instrumental in bringing about some good ideas as to how the game should be played. By his skill as a player and his ability as a golf-course architect, he played an important part in the early days of American golf. As an architect he was the first man to embody into a design of his own other holes he had seen. This he did at the National Golf Links, which was, it is said, America's first really great golf course.

With the formation of a national body, an Amateur Championship was the next step and the first United States Amateur Championship was played at Newport in 1895, the winner being Macdonald.

The U.S. Golf Association started not only the Amateur Championship but also the United States Women's Championship and the United States Open Championship. The Open Championship, played at Newport the day after the Amateur Championship, was won by a young Englishman, Horace Rawlins, who had come there as an assistant professional only nine months previously.

The Women's Championship was held later the same year at the Meadowbrook Club, Hempstead, New York. The first winner was Mrs Charles Brown.

While the amateur and the ladies' game flourished, there were no American professionals of any quality and it was not until 1911 that a home-bred American, J. J. McDermott took the title.

But if the American professionals were slow to start, it was not long before they produced many fine players. By the early 1920s the situation was reversed and their men came to Britain to dominate the British Open Championship. Curiously enough many years before, in 1904, an Australian-born American, Walter Travis, caused a sensation by winning the British Amateur Championship. He did so with a centre-shafted putter of a type outlawed in Britain immediately afterwards. It was banned for many years but is now universally popular.

Just as the centre-shafted putter was invented in the United States, so was the forerunner of the modern golf ball. Before 1901 a ball with a hard centre known as the 'gutty' was used, but in that year Coburn Haskell of Cleveland invented one wound with strips of rubber or elastic and covered with gutta-percha. The first success with the new ball was achieved by Travis in the United States Amateur Championship of 1901 and the first with the Haskell ball in Britain was when Sandy Herd won the British Open a year later.

Travis was one of the great American amateurs, but the best was Robert Tyre Jones who, in 1930, won the two major United States championships and the two major British titles in the same year, a feat not likely to be equalled.

If Jones was the greatest American amateur, perhaps Ben Hogan was the greatest professional, although to compare a golfer of one generation with that of another is dangerous and indeed pointless.

If Sam Snead had managed to win even a single United States Open he would surely have been among the immortals.

Since the early 1920s Americans have more or less dominated world golf, but today they have to face fierce competition. By winning the British Open in 1969 Jacklin gave the game in Britain a big boost.

Australia and South Africa are producing fine players, European golf is becoming stronger and professionals from Japan and other countries in the Far East are making their impact in world-class competition. Many shrewd judges predict that Japan will become the golfing country of the future.

But the United States with so many players and so many golf courses will not lightly give up the leading place they have held for so many years. The contribution American golfers have made is incalculable. Golf has come a long way there since John Reid and his friends set out with their six clubs.

THE IMPLEMENTS OF THE GAME

The maximum number of clubs permitted during a round of golf is fourteen. A golfer beginning with fewer can bring his total to that number and replace a club which has become unfit for play. Neither addition nor replacement can be made by borrowing from any other person playing on the course.

Partners may share clubs provided the total number carried does not exceed fourteen, which is known as a full set and can comprise various combinations of woods and irons. As their names imply, woods and irons have heads made of those respective materials.

Usually a set is made up of four woods, chosen from Nos 1 to 5, nine irons chosen from Nos 1 to 9, a pitching wedge and a sand wedge, there must also be a putter.

Here is a table which gives approximate distances for each club. The distances given are for average players, playing under normal conditions:

	Men	Women
No 1 wood	220 yd (201 m)	185 yd (169 m)
No 2 wood	205 yd (187 m)	175 yd (160 m)
No 3 wood	195 yd (178 m)	165 yd (151 m)
No 4 wood	185 yd (169 m)	160 yd (146 m)
No 5 wood	175 yd (160 m)	145 yd (133 m)
No 1 iron	190 yd (174 m)	160 yd (146 m)
No 2 iron	180 yd (165 m)	150 yd (137 m)
No 3 iron	170 yd (155 m)	140 yd (128 m)
No 4 iron	160 yd (146 m)	130 yd (119 m)
No 5 iron	150 yd (137 m)	120 yd (110 m)
No 6 iron	140 yd (128 m)	110 yd (101 m)
No 7 iron	130 yd (119 m)	100 yd (91 m)
No 8 iron	120 yd (110 m)	90 yd (82 m)
No 9 iron	110 yd (101 m)	80 yd (73 m)
Pitching wedge	100 yd (91 m)	70 yd (64 m)
Sand wedge	90 yd (82 m)	65 yd (59 m)

Each club has its own function. Generally because of the degree of loft on the clubs, those with the lower numbers, i.e. a No 1 wood or No 1 iron propel the ball further than would a No 5 wood or a No 9 iron. The higher numbered clubs being lofted much more than those with low numbers (a No 1 wood has 11 degrees loft, a wedge 55 degrees loft) send the ball higher, with the result that it drops much more quickly than one played with a lower trajectory.

The most powerful club in the bag is the No 1 wood or driver as it is commonly called. This is used for hitting the ball from the teeing ground when it is resting on a wooden or plastic peg. On all other occasions except when winter rules apply (i.e. when the ball can be teed up on the fairway to save wear and tear on the course) the ball is played from where it lies.

The higher the number on the club the shorter the shaft so that the No 1 wood has the longest shaft of all. The same applies to the degree of loft on the club face. The lowest numbers have the least degree of loft.

The most popular material for the shafts of golf clubs is steel, although other materials are used. These include aluminium, glass fibre and the comparatively new carbon fibre. It is claimed for the last named that it gives greater length, and so is becoming increasingly popular in the manufacture of No 1 woods or drivers.

Like all other clubs, the No 1 wood has a 'grip' made of leather or a synthetic material which enables the player to have a good feel or grip.

Top golfers from time to time use the No 1 wood for a shot from the fairway if they feel it is the only club which would send the ball to the green. On such rare occasions the expert satisfies himself that the ball is sitting up enough to enable him to use a club with virtually no degree of loft. Such a shot is not to be recommended for any but the best players.

The No 2 wood is next in the wood range. The head has more loft than the driver and is used for playing long shots from good lies on the fairway. Many golfers, principally those who are in the longer handicap category and who find a driver difficult to play from the tee, use a No 2 wood, sacrificing a little length for greater accuracy. The No 3 wood has more loft still and is highly popular with golfers for fairway shots and occasionally when playing from good lies in the rough. Because it has more loft on the face, its range is not as great as that of the No 2 wood, but also because of its loft it can be played when the ball is not lying well. Many golfers find it a fine utility club.

For most golfers, the No 4 wood is ideal for general purposes. It has yet more loft than the No 3 wood, and this gives many players a feeling of confidence. It can be used for playing

A set of clubs consists of fourteen, usually four woods, nine irons and a putter. The
shot or

off the fairway if the lie is not good, or on occasions from the rough, that is anywhere which is not the fairway, and also when playing against the wind to the green, even though in ordinary circumstances such a shot would normally require an iron club.

As golfers differ in ability, so the distance they hit the ball with any club varies considerably. It is up to the individual golfer to decide his capacity. This is known as 'judgement'. A male golfer who has had some experience should hit the ball from the tee a distance of 200 yd (183 m). Better players can hit the ball much further, but whatever the standard of the player much depends on the prevailing conditions. Obviously the ball can be hit much further downwind than against the wind. It is up to

IRONS - - - - - - →

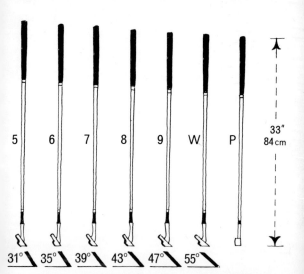

| 5 | 6 | 7 | 8 | 9 | W | P | 33" 84 cm |

31° 35° 39° 43° 47° 55°

clubs (except the putter) vary in the degree of their loft. Each is used for one particular shots

each golfer to decide just how far he can hit the ball with any club. Having established that, then he must select the club, wood or iron, which he thinks is best suited for the task. As beginners cannot hit the ball as far as the experts, they may require a drive and two, sometimes even three, wood shots to reach the precincts of the green.

Like the woods, the iron clubs are graded in relation to their loft; the shafts become shorter and the loft of the faces more pronounced as the number of the club increases. The higher numbered clubs, those with the greatest degree of loft on the face, are used as one nears the green. The reason for this is obvious: with their loft, the ball, when struck, flies higher and

27

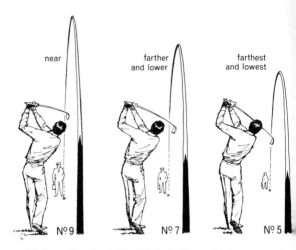

Nº 9

Nº 7

Nº 5

This diagram shows the principle of lofted clubs. The more lofted ones are used for playing high-flying shots as demonstrated by the golfer playing the deep faced No 9 iron. The No 7 is less lofted and the ball does not fly as high. The No 5 flies lower than the shots played by the other two clubs

therefore does not travel as far as it would with an iron having a less lofted face.

The No 1 iron can be discounted since it is not often included in a set these days. It has a very upright face and most people have found it hard to play. However, it is still used by many top professionals and the better amateurs. The No 2 iron has a very slight loft, and apart from the No 1 iron, has a longer shaft than other irons, but it must be emphasized that the length of the shafts varies only slightly.

The No 3 iron is, generally speaking, a fairway club, as is the No 2 iron which can be played for long shots from a good lie and which is especially useful when playing against the wind.

As with all other clubs, only judgment can dictate when to use a No 3 iron, but its chief purpose is to put the ball on the green from a distance of about 170 yd (155 m).

The No 4 iron has more loft than the No 3 and the No 5 iron more than the No 4 and so progressively they are used for shorter shots. Only by playing golf and learning from mistakes can players become efficient. The important point is to know every club in the bag and learn which is the correct one for the shot on hand.

A club like a No 5 or a No 7 iron can also be used for short shots, called chip and run shots, when the player is near the green and there is no obstacle, such as a bunker, intervening. If there is, then the ball has to be lofted over the obstacle with a deep-faced iron, probably the same one as used for recovery shots from bunkers themselves. This can either be a No 9 iron or a comparative newcomer to the golf club family, the wedge.

The wedge is a deep-faced club with a flange on the sole. The idea of the flange is to impart spin on the ball when it lands on the green, which is often necessary. The wedge is a versatile club which can be used for playing out of bunkers and long grass.

It is not necessary, and certainly not for beginners, to have a full set of clubs. Many experts declare that it is better for novices to have only a few clubs at the outset and to become proficient with them before going to the full range.

Most golf professionals and sports shops sell what is called a 'short' set comprised of usually seven clubs, two woods, four irons and a putter. But whether a short set or a full set is being purchased, seek the advice of a golf professional whose business it is to know which clubs suit a particular individual.

A–Z

Cross reference: Words in SMALL CAPITALS refer to entries which may be looked up in this section, unless followed by a page number when the information will be found elsewhere in the book on the page indicated.

Ace American term for a HOLE-IN-ONE.

Address A player is said to have 'addressed the ball' when he has taken up his stance in order to play a shot, and has GROUNDED HIS CLUB. Grounding the club is not permitted in a BUNKER, however.

Advice In a competition or a match a player may take advice only from his partner, his caddie or his partner's caddie. If he takes advice from anyone else he is penalized. This means that he either loses the hole or if it is a stroke play competition he must add two shots to his score for the hole.

Air shot (fresh air shot) When a player in attempting a stroke completely misses the ball. Although the ball has not been moved, the player must count one stroke.

Albatross A score of three under PAR for a hole. Thus if the hole is a par five and the player has HOLED OUT in two strokes he is deemed to have scored an albatross. The terms relating to holes done in a score below par are all concerned with birds. Three under par is the biggest under par score possible in normal conditions, and the albatross, being a large bird, is the term used in this instance.

All flat *See* ALL SQUARE.

Alliances Throughout Britain there are golfing alliances (societies) which in the main run competitions during the winter. Generally professionals team up with amateurs. The Croydon and District Alliance in Surrey claims to have been the first and other golfers in districts all over Britain have followed suit.

All square (All flat) The term used in MATCH PLAY when a match is level at any stage, including the finish. 'All flat' is used in the same way.

Alnmouth *See* FAMOUS BRITISH CLUBS AND COURSES p. 145.

Aluminium shafts Shafts made of this material have had some success in the United States. Efforts were made to introduce them into Britain but they did not achieve much popularity mainly because they had a dull finish, were thicker than steel shafts, and were more expensive. Until new manufacturing techniques are evolved to enable the shafts to be made more attractive and sold at a cheaper price, it is unlikely they will oust steel shafts in popularity.

Amateur According to the Rules of Golf an amateur is one who plays golf solely as a non-remunerative or non-profit-making sport. (*See also* AMATEUR STATUS.)

Amateur Internationals The first amateur golf international was played in 1902 on the course of the Royal Liverpool Club at Hoylake, Cheshire, between England and Scotland. The teams were ten a side and Scotland won by 32 holes to 25 holes. The England versus Scotland match continued for 30 years when Ireland and Wales were brought in to make a quadrilateral event.

Amateur status The rules governing amateur golfers are very strict. Set out below (together with some exceptions) are several of the more important acts which violate the definition of an amateur golfer, and which if carried out would cause a player to lose his amateur status, and thus be barred from all kinds of amateur competitions:

'Receiving payment or compensation for acting as a professional golfer in any capacity.

'Receiving payment or compensation for giving instruction in playing golf, either orally, in writing, by pictures or by other demonstrations, to either individuals or groups.

'Exceptions are granted to physical training and other teachers whose scholastic duties include giving sports tuition to pupils at recognized educational establishments.

'Playing for prize money in a match, tournament or exhibition.

'Accepting a prize or testimonial which has a retail value greater than fifty pounds. (N.B. now £100).

'Receiving payment for a personal appearance because of golf skill or reputation.

'Receiving or contracting to receive payment of compensa-

31

tion directly or indirectly for allowing one's name to be advertised or published as the author of golf articles or books of which he is not actually the author.

'Because of golf skill or reputation receiving payment or compensation directly or indirectly for promoting the sale of golf merchandise at either whole or retail level.

'Accepting golf balls, clubs, golf merchandise, golf clothing or golf shoes at under the current market price.'

Amateur golfers are forbidden to accept expenses for any purpose connected with golf, with certain exceptions.

American golf, History of   *See* HISTORY OF AMERICAN GOLF, p. 19.

American tournament   A competition in which every competitor plays all the other entrants. Sometimes referred to as a 'Round Robin' tournament.

Apple Tree Gang   The name given to the pioneers of golf in the United States, so called because they played on what was an apple orchard. (*See also* HISTORY OF AMERICAN GOLF, p. 20.)

Apron of the green   The area of the fairway just short of the green. The grass within this area is usually cut shorter than the grass on the rest of the fairway.

Arc (of the swing)   The circular groove in which the head of a golf club moves during the swing.

Artisan   Artisan or as they were originally defined—working men golfers—can play at many clubs within certain specified times. The artisans are provided or provide themselves with their own club house. They run their own competitions and pay a subscription to the parent club, a subscription which is very much smaller than that paid by ordinary members. The oldest artisan club in England is said to be the Bulwell Forest Artisans Club, Nottingham, which was formed in 1887. A year later the famous Northam Working Men's Club was founded at Northam in Devon.

Augusta National   *See* FAMOUS AMERICAN CLUBS, p. 153.

Avia Ladies' International   One of the most important of women's events. It started in 1966 and is organized by the firm of Louis Newmark which also stages the Newmark International.

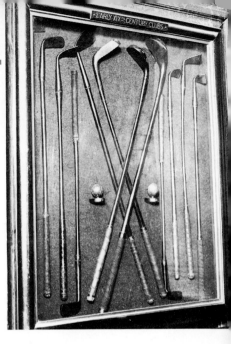

(*right*) Early 19th-century clubs and two golf balls, dated 1718 and 1848, at the Royal Blackheath Club at Eltham, near London. The balls have a leather cover and are packed with compressed feathers

(*left*) A ball made of gutta-percha followed the one filled with feathers. The gutta ball, as it was called, came into being about 1848 and stayed until replaced by the rubber-cored ball in 1902

(*above*) A historic picture of the young American amateur, Francis Ouimet (*centre*), with the British professionals Harry Vardon (*left*) and Ted Ray (*right*), after he had beaten them in a play-off for the U.S. Open Championship in 1913

(*left*) The most popular grip in golf, the Vardon grip. It is demonstrated here by the great Robert T. Jones, Jun.

(*above*) The amazing thing is that the early lady golfers were able to play so well considering their voluminous clothes and large hats. This is a group at an early championship. (*below left*) One of the leading American professional golfers, Jerry Heard, dressed in the modern style adopted by many players. (*below right*) The modern style again. Mrs Jan Dorrestein, wife of the Dutch professional, frequently acts as his caddy

Back door (tradesman's entrance) Occasionally when a player putts on an undulating green, the ball rolls round the hole and enters it from the back. This is called 'going in the back door' or tradesman's entrance.

Back nine An American expression meaning the last nine holes on a golf course (the same as second nine).

Backspin When the ball, having been played to the green, usually with a deep-faced iron, strikes the grass and spins backwards it is said to have backspin. Professionals are very good at this shot but less practised players find it hard to accomplish. The art is in hitting the ball with a descending blow.

Backswing The movement by which the hands and arms take the club back before bringing it down to strike the ball.

Baffy The old term for the wooden club which was in many respects similar to a No 3 or No 4 wood club in today's range. In the early days of the game this club was sometimes referred to as a 'baffing spoon'.

Ball *See* GOLF BALL, HISTORY OF.

Ball at rest When the ball has come to a stop it is said to be 'at rest'.

Ball dropped In accordance with the rules for a ball out of bounds, a lost ball or an unplayable ball, it is permissible to drop a ball so that the game can continue. There is a correct procedure for dropping a ball. 'He shall face the hole, stand erect and drop the ball behind him over his shoulder.' (Rule 22 of the Rules of Golf.)

Ball holed A ball is 'holed' when it lies within the circumference of the hole and all of it is below the level of the lip of the hole.

Ball in play A ball is in play immediately it has been struck off the tee and until it rests in the hole, except when it is out of bounds, lost or lifted. The term 'keeping the ball in play' generally means that the striker keeps it out of HAZARDS or unplayable LIES and remains within the boundaries of the course.

Ball lost The Rules of Golf allow five minutes search for a lost ball. The player or his side or their caddies are entitled to look for the ball and usually the opponent also helps in the search.

Ball mark The term used in the Rules of Golf for the mark made when the ball lands on the green. The player is entitled to and indeed should be encouraged to repair any indentation so caused. In doing so he can lift the ball, replacing it on the same spot.

Ball moved A ball is deemed to have moved if it leaves its original position. If the player accidentally moves the ball whether he has addressed it or not, he incurs a penalty of one stroke. A one-stroke penalty is also imposed if the ball is moved when a player clears away loose material such as stones, leaves or sticks. The Rules of Golf also cover instances where a ball is moved by an opponent or by an opponent's ball. In the former instance the opponent suffers a penalty of one stroke but there is no penalty in the latter case.

Ball played as it lies That the ball should be played wherever it comes to rest is one of the earliest and most fundamental rules of the game. It does not now apply to the same extent as it did. If there is a doubt whether or not the ball can be lifted it is best to play the ball 'as it lies'.

Baltusrol *See* FAMOUS AMERICAN CLUBS, p. 153.

Bandit (hustler) Describes a golfer who plays off what is suspected to be a wrong or 'phoney' handicap. Known as a HUSTLER in the United States.

Belt (Open Championship) When the Open Championship was inaugurated in 1860 by the Prestwick Club the winner was presented with an ornate silver belt to be held for one year. There was a proviso that if the same man won the belt in three successive years it would become his property. Young Tom Morris did this in the years 1868, 1869 and 1870, so the belt which had been presented by the Earl of Eglinton became his own. After his success there was a lapse in the championship of one year and then the present silver trophy was presented. The trophy was subscribed for by the Prestwick Club, the Royal and Ancient Golf Club and the Honourable Company of Edinburgh Golfers. The value of the belt and the silver trophy was approximately the same—£30. (*See also* BRITISH OPEN CHAMPIONSHIP.)

Best ball competition A form of friendly match in which one player plays the best ball of three others.

Better ball competition   A form of stroke competition in which two partners play as a team, the better score of each player counting at each hole. Also used when one player plays against the better ball of two other players.

Birdie   The term used when a player has HOLED OUT in one under the PAR score of a hole.

Biggest wins   The biggest win in golf would seem to be that of Allan Robertson against Willie Dunn in 1843. The match was over 20 rounds and Robertson won by 2 rounds up and 1 to play.

In 1928 Archie Compston, the British professional, beat Walter Hagen of the United States in a 72-hole match by 18 HOLES UP and 17 to play.

In the 1934 British Amateur Championship final Lawson Little of the United States beat James Wallace, a local golfer, by 14 up and 13 to play. The final was over 36 holes. Almost immediately Wallace turned professional, and was successful as such.

Bisque   The equivalent of a stroke in a once popular form of play. It is a system of handicapping in which the player in receipt of a certain number of bisques or strokes can nominate the holes at which he takes them. He can say that he wishes to take a bisque after the hole has been played. Usually a player does so after he has halved a hole to turn it into a win. The number of bisques conceded is fewer than the strokes under normal handicapping.

Blairgowrie   *See* FAMOUS BRITISH CLUBS AND COURSES, p. 145.

Blaster   Name given many years ago to the broadsoled club used for recovery shots from BUNKERS. It is still used today for such clubs as the sand wedge, wedge or deep-faced niblick. (*See also* SAND IRON.)

Blind hole or shot   A blind hole is so-called when the green cannot be seen from the teeing ground. A blind shot is played when some undulation of the ground or hazard prevents the player from having a clear sight of the green.

Bogey   In general terms this means the SCRATCH value of a hole or a course, or in the early days, the GROUND SCORE. Several clubs claim to have originated this term, but it is generally agreed that the Great Yarmouth Club at least had a part in its initiation, if not the actual system. Before that time there appears to have been in use at the Elie Club in Scotland a ground score. At the Coventry Club there was not only a ground score but the members competed against it. But at that time no title had been given to the competition and the name came into being at the Great Yarmouth Club which also had a ground score.

About that time (1890) there was a popular song, 'Hush, hush, hush. Here comes the bogey man.' One day the secretary of the club, Dr Thomas Browne, was playing with a Major Charles Wellman in a competition against the ground score. The good doctor was in some trouble and his partner exclaimed, 'This opponent of yours is a regular bogey man.' The name was then adopted by the club for all future competitions of this type.

Later Dr Browne was at a club in Hampshire, the now defunct United Services Club at Alverstoke, where he said he wished to introduce a new member who was a steady golfer hard to beat. As it was a Services club he gave the new member, i.e. the bogey, the rank of colonel.

The term bogey, referring to the score which a scratch player was expected to take at each hole or for the course, has to a large extent been superseded by the term PAR for each hole and by STANDARD SCRATCH SCORE for the course. Many clubs still use the term bogey. The bogey score is rather more lenient than the STANDARD SCRATCH SCORE.

Bogey (American version) In the United States the term bogey is used when a player takes one over PAR at a hole. A double bogey is two over par, a treble bogey three over par and so on. This term seems to have sprung from a mistaken idea that in Britain bogey meant one stroke over par.

Bogey competitions In a competition played against bogey (or par) a player receives three-quarters of his handicap and counts the holes he is up or down against the bogey (or par) of the course. In such a competition the player is required to put down his score at every hole, thus plus for a win, zero for a half and minus for a loss.

Bold A term used usually in putting to describe a shot when the ball has been hit past the hole. It is also used for approach shots which have finished either on the green past the hole or have gone over the green altogether.

Bolt (a putt)   When a player has sent the ball into the hole at express speed, it is sometimes said that 'he bolted the putt'.

Boundary   The perimeter of a golf course beyond which if a ball is played, a player is deemed to be out of bounds.

Bowf (woof)   The word is an old Scots one meaning bark (as of a dog). In friendly games, but not so much now, players agreed that an opponent would have the right to utter a loud ejaculation as another player was about to play for the purpose of upsetting the striker. A player would be given the right to use a 'bowf' or 'woof' a limited number of times. But it was not only the fact of hearing the noise which caused players to be upset, but waiting for the noise which never came. A 'woof' is used by Americans as a handicap.

Boyd Quaich Tournament   An open annual stroke play tournament over 72 holes for university students in Britain and overseas. The quaich (Scots for porridge bowl) was presented for competition by Professor and Mrs Boyd in memory of their two student sons who lost their lives in World War II. It is always played at St Andrews.

Brabazon Trophy   Given by the late Lord Brabazon for amateur competition. The tournament is now known as the ENGLISH OPEN AMATEUR STROKE PLAY CHAMPIONSHIP.

Brae Burn   *See* FAMOUS AMERICAN CLUBS, p. 153.

Braid, James   *See* TRIUMVIRATE, THE GREAT.

Brassie (or brassey)   The old name for a No 2 wood. The club had a brass sole, and a face laid back so that it could be used for playing FAIRWAY shots.

British Amateur Championship   The man who was the 'father' of the Amateur Championship was Thomas Owen Potter, a Hoylake golfer who thought it would be a fine thing if an Open competition for amateur golfers were to be held on the Hoylake links. He arranged it for 1885 and the winner from a field of 48 competitors was a local player, A. F. Macfie, who was a native of St Andrews. The Hoylake golfers were delighted with the success of their meeting and at once approached the Royal and Ancient Club to enquire whether anybody might be interested in organizing an official championship and the answer was 'yes'. A tentative enquiry on the same lines had been made in 1877, but then the Royal and Ancient would have nothing to do with the suggestion. By 1885, when the Hoylake golfers stepped in, the officials at St Andrews no doubt realized they had made a mistake. Twenty-four leading clubs subscribed £100 to purchase the trophy, one of the finest silver trophies in sport. It is held by the winner for one year. The first official Amateur Championship (under the auspices of the Royal and Ancient club) was held in 1886, the venue naturally being St Andrews. The twenty-four clubs mentioned assisted in the organization in the early years and the only courses used were Hoylake, St Andrews and Prestwick. Other venues followed in 1892, the first of these being Royal St George's, Sandwich. Of the courses which have housed the Amateur Championship only one, Ganton in Yorkshire, is inland. It was the venue for the 1964 championship.

Each match played in the championship is played over 18 holes except the final which is contested over 36. Players must have a handicap of two strokes or less and entry is limited to 256 competitors. In the event of applications exceeding this number, entry for the higher handicap competitors shall be decided by ballot. Full particulars of conditions of entry can be had from the Secretary, Championship Committee, *Royal and Ancient Golf Club,* St Andrews, Scotland. (For winners *see* p. 175.)

British Amateur Champions   Outstanding Amateur champions have been John Ball who won the Amateur Championship more times than any other golfer, taking the title eight times in all, in 1888, 1890, 1892, 1894, 1899, 1907, 1910 and 1912. He also won the Open Championship in 1890. Michael Bonallack has won the Amateur Championship five times, in 1961, 1965, 1968, 1969 and 1970. Harold Hilton won the Amateur Championship four times, the Open Championship twice, and the United States Amateur Championship once. Joe Carr won the Amateur Championship three times.

British Boys' Amateur Championship   The championship began in 1921, the two men involved in its start being Mr Donald Mathieson, owner of the magazine *Golf Monthly*, and Lt Col South of Sutton Coldfield. In 1949 the Royal and Ancient Club took control. The championship is for amateur boy golfers of under 18 years of age and whose handicap is not more than six strokes. It is a match play event and the venues vary each year. There is no qualifying test. The winner holds the challenge trophy for one year and receives a golf medal. The runner-up receives a silver medal and the two semi-finalists a bronze medal. Full particulars of conditions of entry can be had from the Secretary, Championship Committee, *Royal and Ancient Golf Club,* St Andrews, Scotland.

British Championships: First overseas winners   In 1904 Walter J. Travis, an Australian-born American, won the *British Amateur Championship* at Sandwich.

In 1907 Arnaud Massy, a Frenchman, won the *British Open Championship* at Hoylake.

In 1970 Baldovino Dassu of Italy won the *Youths' British Open Amateur Championship* at Barnton.

In 1928 S. Scheftel, an American based at Le Touquet in France, won the *British Boys' Amateur Championship* at Formby.

In 1927 Mlle Thion de la Chaume won the *British Ladies' Open Amateur Championship* at Newcastle, County Down. She married the famous tennis player, René Lacoste, and their daughter Catherine won the title in 1969.

British Girls' Open Amateur Championship   This match play championship, run originally by a women's magazine, was inaugurated in 1919. It is open to all girl amateur golfers under the age of 19. For twenty years the championship was held at Stoke Poges Golf Club near Slough, but now the venues are spread over the country and it is run by the LADIES' GOLF UNION annually. Matches are over 18 holes. There is no handicap limit. Particulars can be obtained from the Secretary, Ladies' Golf Union, 11, The Links, St Andrews, Fife, Scotland.

British Ladies' Open Amateur Championship   After Miss Izette Pearson and her friends at Wimbledon (with the aid of Mr W. Laidlaw Purvis) had formed the LADIES' GOLF UNION, it was only a step to holding a championship. At St Annes, where women golfers had their own course, the ladies had a similar idea and had in fact inaugurated an Open competition for which they had a trophy. It was decided to have a new trophy subscribed for by the founder clubs of the union, and that the venue for the first championship would be St Annes.

On 13th June 1893, the same year that the Ladies' Golf Union was formed, the first championship was played over 18 holes. Thirty-eight ladies with big hats, loose skirts and tight corsets entered, and the winner was Lady Margaret Scott who beat Miss Pearson in the final by 7 and 5 (7 HOLES UP and 5 to play). The same two met in the final the following year at Littlestone and Lady Margaret Scott won again. She won the following year and then retired. She was a member of a famous golfing family.

So far only two other women have won the championship three times in succession, Miss Cecil Leitch and Miss Enid Wilson. The championship has produced many personalities and many outstanding players but it is generally conceded that Lady Heathcoat Amory (Miss Joyce Wethered) was the greatest woman golfer of all time. She won the title four times in all but retired from competitive golf after her last championship victory.

The championship consists of 18-hole qualifying rounds (stroke play) on each of two days. The leading players (16, 32 or 64 depending on the number of entries) then qualify for match play. Entries are only accepted from women amateur golfers who have a certified handicap of six or under, the entry of the 128 lowest handicaps to be accepted and a ballot for the last places if necessary. Full particulars of conditions of entry can be obtained from the Secretary, Ladies' Golf Union, 11, The Links, St Andrews, Fife, Scotland. (For winners see p. 177.)

British Ladies' Amateur Stroke Play Championship Played over 72 holes. It was inaugurated in 1969. (See also STROKE PLAY.) The event consists of qualifying rounds of 18 holes on each of two days. The leading 32 competitors, decided on the lowest number of strokes played, then play a further 36 holes. Conditions of entry can be obtained from the Secretary, Ladies' Golf Union, 11, The Links, St Andrews, Fife, Scotland.

British Open Championship Around the middle of the last century the Prestwick Club in Ayrshire had engaged the great Tom Morris of St Andrews as green-keeper. By then his reputation as a player was considerable and so proud were the club members of his prowess that they felt he should be pitted against other professionals in order to prove to the golfing public at large that their man was the best.

The idea for such a competition was first mooted in 1856 but the first competition was not played until 1860. For this, the club put up a grand championship belt of silver, suitably ornamented, to be held by the winner for one year with the proviso that if a player won it three years in succession it would be his own property. This generous gesture was later to create a crisis.

It was decided that the tournament should consist of three rounds—27 holes in all—and on the appointed day eight competitors carrying their few clubs under their arms appeared. But Prestwick members, hoping that Tom Morris would romp home, were disappointed, for the winner was Willie Park, Senior, of Musselburgh, whose total was 174.

But Tom Morris, Senior, won the following year, and the event became an annual one at Prestwick though it created little notice. Then in 1868 the winner was Tom Morris, Junior, who won the next two years to make the belt his own. That caused confusion, so much so that in 1871 no competition was held. Discussions between the Prestwick Club, the Honourable Company of Edinburgh Golfers and the Royal and Ancient Club resulted in these clubs putting up the present cup for competition. It was decided that the event would be played in turn on the links of the three clubs and that the first would be at Prestwick. This brought another victory for 'Young Tommy' but it was his last. Three years later, on Christmas Day in 1875, he died of pneumonia.

1890 was a landmark of the championship because it was won for the first time by an Englishman. He was John Ball of Hoylake. That win perhaps gave the championship a wider appeal and in 1892 it was decided that it should be played over 72 holes. The winner was again an amateur also from Hoylake, Harold Hilton. By now an entrance fee of ten shillings was imposed and the three organizing clubs subscribed £15 each. Prize money which had begun at £5 was now increased to £100, the winner receiving the trophy, a gold medal and £30. The first to benefit from this big increase was Willie Auchterlonie of St Andrews. He was the last winner before the Great Triumvirate, Braid, Taylor and Vardon, came to dominate the championship, as they did for a period of 20 years. Taylor, the winner in 1894, was the first English professional to be champion.

The championship continued without a break until 1914

when World War I caused an interruption. It was resumed in 1920 when George Duncan won at Deal which had been introduced as a venue in 1909, as had Sandwich (1894) and Hoylake (1897). Muirfield, the new home of the Honourable Company, had been used since 1892.

World War I had changed many things and it changed the face of the Open Championship for in 1921 Jock Hutchison became the first man from across the Atlantic to win. British successes in the years between the wars and after were pitifully few, Henry Cotton (three times) being the outstanding British champion.

Americans began to dominate the scene in the 1920s with the great amateur, Bobby Jones, perhaps their most outstanding player. In later decades other overseas players such as Bobby Locke and Peter Thomson stole some of the limelight from the Americans. The feats of two Americans, however, deserve to be recorded, for Hogan (1953) and the late Tony Lema (1964) both won at their first attempt. Lema's astonishing win at St Andrews following a late arrival and no full practice round was perhaps one of the most amazing of all Open Championship victories. And if Lema's was one of the most astounding, that of the 44-year-old Argentinian, Roberto de Vicenzo in 1967, was the most emotional. He was the oldest man ever to win the championship and the great reception given to him was a memorable one, only equalled perhaps by the win of Britain's Tony Jacklin at Royal Lytham in 1969, the first home player to take the title since Max Faulkner in 1951.

There has been emotion, too, at championships when a favourite of the crowd has lost with victory seemingly in his grasp. Doug Sanders at St Andrews in 1970 was faced with a putt of less than a yard on the last green at St Andrews to win. He missed to tie with Nicklaus who won in the PLAY-OFF.

Vardon's six wins still stand as the record for the most victories in the championship.

The championship which is decided by stroke play is played over 72 holes each year. There are qualifying rounds and the number of qualifiers totals 150. After 54 holes the leading sixty competitors and all those tying for 60th place complete the championship. Venues vary.

The event is open to professional golfers and also to men amateur golfers with a handicap of one or less. Conditions of entry can be obtained from the Secretary, Championship Committee, *Royal and Ancient Golf Club,* St Andrews, Scotland. The prize money for the 1974 British Open Championship was £50,000; for 1975 £75,000. (For winners *see* p. 172.)

British Open Championship courses   The following courses have been the venue of the championship:

Carnoustie—1931, 1937, 1953, 1968, 1975

Muirfield—1892, 1896, 1901, 1906, 1912, 1929, 1935, 1948, 1959, 1966, 1972.

Musselburgh—1874, 1877, 1880, 1883, 1886, 1889.

Prestwick—1860–70, 1872, 1875, 1878, 1881, 1884, 1887, 1890, 1893, 1898, 1903, 1908, 1914, 1925.

Princes—1932.

Royal Birkdale—1954, 1961, 1965, 1971, 1976.

Royal Cinque Ports—1909, 1920.

Royal Liverpool—1897, 1902, 1907, 1913, 1924, 1930, 1936, 1947, 1956, 1967.

Royal Lytham and St Annes—1926, 1952, 1958, 1963, 1969, 1974.

Royal Portrush—1951.

Royal St George's—1894, 1899, 1904, 1911, 1922, 1928, 1934, 1938, 1949.

St Andrews—1873, 1876, 1879, 1882, 1885, 1888, 1891, 1895, 1900, 1905, 1910, 1921, 1927, 1933, 1939, 1946, 1955, 1957, 1960, 1964, 1970.

Troon—1923, 1950, 1962, 1973.

Turnberry—1977.

British Open Championship: Highest winning total   326 (72 holes), J. H. Taylor at Royal St George's, Sandwich in 1894.

British Open Championship: Largest entry   679 players entered in 1974.

British Open Championship: Lowest entry   Eight players entered for the first three championships and the same number played in 1872, the first championship for the silver trophy.

British Open Championship: Lowest round   65. T. H. Cotton, St George's, Sandwich—1934; E. C. Brown, Royal Lytham—1958; L. Ruiz, Royal Lytham—1958; P. J. Butler, Muirfield—1966; C. O'Connor, Royal Lytham—1969; N. C. Coles, St Andrews—1970.

British Open Championship: Lowest winning total 272 (72 holes). Arnold Palmer at Troon in 1962.

British Open Championship: Oldest winners Roberto de Vicenzo is the oldest man to have won the championship. He was 44 years and 93 days when he won at Hoylake in 1967. Harry Vardon, when he won his sixth title at Prestwick in 1914, was 44 years, 42 days.

British Open Championship: Youngest winner 'Young Tommy' Morris was 18 when he won the championship at Prestwick in 1868.

British Professional Match Play Championship This event which began in 1903 and was sponsored by the *News of the World* became the British Professional Match Play Championship in 1946. Among many famous winners were James Braid and Dai Rees who each won the event four times. After 1969 the *News of the World* ceased to be controlled by the Carr family and the event was taken over by the Long John Scotch Whisky firm. That lasted only one year and then in 1970 it was allowed to lapse. Then for three years the Benson and Hedges tobacco organization sponsored the event annually.

Brookline Country Club (Country Club of Brookline) *See* FAMOUS AMERICAN CLUBS, p. 153; HISTORY OF AMERICAN GOLF, p. 20.

Bruntsfield Links Golfing Society *See* FAMOUS BRITISH CLUBS AND COURSES, p. 145.

Bunker A hollow on the course filled with sand termed a HAZARD. Bunkers can be found at strategic points on a FAIRWAY and at the back or sides of a green for trapping an inaccurate shot. Bunkers first came into being on seaside courses by reason of golf balls landing in hollows. As a result, with so many shots being played from near the same spot, in time the grass disappeared leaving only sand. Now bunkers are man-made. (*See also* GRASS BUNKERS.)

Burma Road The name coined to describe the West Course of the Wentworth Club in Surrey. The name is derived from the infamous wartime track through the jungle in Burma during World War II.

Burnham and Berrow *See* FAMOUS BRITISH CLUBS AND COURSES, p. 145.

Bye   The number of holes of a round remaining to be played when a match has ended. Often there is a little wager on who can win the bye or remaining holes.

Caddie   The caddie is not as familiar a figure on golf courses as he once was, but there are still professional caddies, most of whom carry the clubs of golfers in tournaments. When not doing so they are usually engaged in carrying the clubs of golf club members. A few top caddies are employed full time by the golf stars, mostly working on a retainer and a bonus system tied to their employer's winnings. The word 'caddie' is derived from the French word, 'cadet' a young messenger. The word was brought to Scotland by members of the entourage of Mary Queen of Scots and 'Cadets' (or boys) were engaged in carrying errands.

Caddies, as a whole, are great characters, and many of them during the years have become good golfers. Indeed most of the early professionals began as caddies. Now, in the days of big money, caddying is a very professional business and calls for a high degree of skill where a caddie can assist his master to play the shots he desires. This is in addition to carrying the heavy bag of clubs and between tournaments keeping his master's equipment in good order.

Caddie car   Another name for golf trolley. This is a wheeled metal frame on which a golfer puts his clubs and wheels them round the course. Caddie cars or trolleys are comparatively new. Most are pulled by hand but there are (mostly in United States) mechanically propelled caddie cars popularly called 'buggies'.

Calamity Jane   The name given to the putter which became famous in the hands of American golfer Robert Tyre Jones. The original 'Calamity Jane' was a lady who it is said became a legend of the old Wild West for smoothing out the problems of various men in her life. As this particular putter smoothed out problems for its owner it was given the name 'Calamity Jane'. It was presented to Jones by an exiled Scot named Maiden.

Callaway System   This form of handicapping is widely used in America but not on a wide scale in Britain. Lionel Callaway was born in Hampshire and emigrated to the United States in 1913. He became a well-known professional and finished his active career at Pinehurst, North Carolina, where he now resides. While at the Bradford Country Club he realized that many golfers who attended conventions and competed in the attendant golf competitions came from all over the country and this made handicapping difficult. So Callaway decided to introduce his system whereby a player's handicap is determined after each round by deducting from his score for the 18 holes the strokes taken for the worst holes during the first 16. The number of 'worst' holes which can be deducted can vary from none for a man who has gone round in par to six holes for a man who has gone round in an astronomical number of strokes. For instance, if a player's worst three holes up to the 16th are 9, 8 and 7, his handicap is 24.

Cambuta or cambuca   Another game where a ball was hit with a club played in England about the 14th century. In Gloucester Cathedral there is a stained-glass window showing a man swinging a club of the kind used in cambutta. It is believed that this picture dates from the 14th century but little more is known of it than that. (*See also* CHOLE, PALL MALL, PAGANICA.)

Canada Cup (now World Cup)   This trophy now known as the WORLD CUP, was given by a wealthy Canadian industrialist, John J. Hopkins, for competition among the professional golfers of the world playing as national teams to further good relationships between golfers of all countries.

Carnoustie   A famous golf course in Scotland, known particularly for its length and the testing challenge it offers. The town itself, however, is even more famous for the enormous number of golfers it has sent to the United States and overseas. Many of them have become renowned teachers of the game. (*See also* FAMOUS BRITISH CLUBS AND COURSES, p. 145.)

Carris Trophy   This competition is open to boys under 18 and was founded by a great enthusiast, Mr Austin Carris. So far, it has always been played at Moor Park Golf Club, Hertfordshire.

Carry   The distance the ball travels on leaving the club to the spot where it pitches.

Casual water   A water HAZARD. If the ball is hit into a pool caused by rain it can be lifted without penalty. If the accumulation of water is not visible, but appears as the golfer takes his stance, a LIFT AND DROP WITHOUT PENALTY is still permissible.

Centre-shafted putter   A putter where the shaft is joined to the club-head in the centre, and not at one end, as was the case with earlier putters. The centre-shafted putter is now universally used by golfers.

Championships: highest scores   An alleged American professional, Walter Danecki, playing in the qualifying test of the British Open Championship at Hillside, Southport, in 1965, scored 108 in the first round and 113 in his second round. That scoring represented 83 over par. He failed to qualify!

Championships: most putts   Six putts on the fifth green at Oakmont by American professional, Dave Hill, in 1962.

Championship winners: most times   Harry Vardon won the British Open Championship six times. James Braid, J. H. Taylor and Peter Thomson have won it five times.

Ronnie Shade, now a professional, won the Scottish Amateur Championship five years in a row from 1963 to 1967.

Ben Hogan won the United States Open Championship four times.

Cheating   In golf the penalties for cheating are severe and can include expulsion from the club, or if a professional exclusion from membership of Professional Golfers' Association of which he may be a member.

Chicago   *See* FAMOUS AMERICAN CLUBS, p. 154.

Chip or chip shot   A little lofted shot to the green. It is employed mainly to lift the ball over a bunker, rough ground, or some other HAZARD which lies between the player and the green.

Chole   An early ball game played in the Low Countries a century before golf was known in Scotland. It was played as a cross-country game, and not in a confined space.

Cleek   The old Scottish name for a club which has now become obsolete. The loft on the face was rather similar to the No 2 iron of today, but the face was a good deal narrower which made it a particularly versatile club for play from the fairway and also from the rough.

Closed stance   The position at ADDRESS when the left foot is pushed forward beyond the intended flight of the ball. If the ball is hit correctly it will go to the right of the target. Such action

The first green on the Queen's course at Gleneagles, with the famous hotel in the background. One of Scotland's great golfing resorts

(*above*) The Blairgowrie Club's course at Rosemount is acknowledged to be one of the finest inland courses in Britain. This is the first green looking back towards the clubhouse.

(*below*) A picturesque view of one of the greens at Killarney. The lake, famous in song and story, is in the background

There are two fine and picturesque courses at the Berkshire Club near Ascot. This is the second hole on the Red Course

may be desirable to avoid a hazard. Some golfers who have a tendency to hit the ball to the left sometimes adopt a closed stance to counteract their fault. (*See also* STANCE and OPEN STANCE.)

Club-Head　That part of the club with which the ball is stuck and to which the shaft is joined.

Club-Head covers or hoods　Specially designed equipment for the protection of the heads of wooden clubs and sometimes putters. They are made of various materials from synthetic to mink!

Clubs　(1) The instruments with which the ball is struck. No golfer is permitted to carry more than fourteen clubs during a round of golf. The choice is left to the individual player, and golf can be played with any number of clubs, fewer than fourteen. The figure 'fourteen' is purely an arbitrary one and was brought into the rules because in the period following World War I, some players carried enormous numbers.

(2) The term 'club' can also refer to the place at which golf is played. (*See also* THE IMPLEMENTS OF THE GAME, p. 24.)

Cocking the wrists　For a golf ball to be hit with any degree of efficiency the club-head has first to be taken back as close to the ground as possible. When it cannot be taken back any further the next stage in the SWING is for the club-head to be forced upwards. This can only be done if cocking or bending of the wrists takes place.

Commonwealth Tournament (Ladies)　Played every four years between teams of women golfers from Commonwealth countries for a trophy presented by Viscountess Astor. The first tournament was held at St Andrews in 1959. It is played in each competing country in turn.

Competitions: highest rounds　316 by Von Cittern at Biarritz in 1888. In a competition in the United States, John Murphy returned a score of 298.

Concede　(1) A hole is conceded or given up when one player has played so many strokes that it is impossible to win it from his opponent. He then picks up his ball and indicates to the opponent that he has given up the hole.

(2) To concede a putt is to regard that the ball will be holed by the next stroke.

Courses: most played on   An American golfer, Ralph Kennedy, claimed to have played on 3615 courses. He gave up golf in 1953.

Council of National Golf Unions   C.O.N.G.U. was inaugurated in 1924 as a result of a meeting between the Royal and Ancient Club and the four home golf unions. The council is made up of two representatives from each union and it manages various aspects of the game in so far as it concerns amateurs in Britain and Ireland. One of its functions is to organize the home international matches and to co-ordinate dates for the leading amateur golf events.

County Championships   Each county in Britain has its separate associations to look after the affairs of men's and women's golf and organizes county championships for both sexes.

Course   The area on which golf is played. A golf course usually has 18 holes, but there are also many nine-hole courses which are played over twice to make up the 18 holes. Nine-hole courses are built where there is insufficient land to make what is termed 'the full circuit'. Courses consist of TEES, FAIRWAYS, GREENS, ROUGH and other HAZARDS, some natural, others man-made.

Crail   *See* FAMOUS BRITISH CLUBS AND COURSES, p. 146.

Curtis Cup   A competition played every two years between the amateur women golfers of Great Britain and Ireland, and the United States. The Cup was donated for competition between the women golfers of these countries by the sisters Margaret and Harriet Curtis, who were famous American golfers at the turn of the century. The first Curtis Cup match was played in 1932 in England at the Wentworth Golf Club and since then it has been played alternatively in Britain and the United States.

Cut   *See* SLICE.

Cut-up shot   Not so often seen nowadays, this was a stroke in which the player drew the club-face across the ball from the outside to inside, thus causing the ball to rise abruptly. Now with the advent of modern clubs, half shots and improvised shots are no longer called for, so the cut-up shot is virtually a thing of the past.

Dead (ball)   The ball is said to be 'dead' when it stops so near the hole that it is felt the putt cannot be missed. Since in golf nothing is certain, there is no specific distance for ruling a ball dead or not dead. It is up to a player's opponent to pronounce a ball 'dead' and so concede the putt. In all competitions except match play it is obligatory to HOLE OUT, since the final result depends on the best score of all entrants.

Dimples   The average golf ball according to manufacturers has 333 dimples. There is no particular reason for the 333, and this has presumably been decided on for technical reasons. The depth of each dimple is 0.0135 in (0.34425 mm). In early days golf balls were smooth but after the advent of the *gutta* golfers discovered that they flew much further after they had been marked by blows from clubs, so they marked the balls by hitting them with a hammer. Later golf balls became marked by regular patterns, squares, and the like. Eventually the makers settled on dimples as the most efficient markings, but experiments proceed continually to find other efficient markings.

Direction posts   Posts are erected on golf courses to indicate the correct line which the player should take to play a shot to a green which is hidden from view. On occasions, a tall direction post is erected at the back of a green to indicate the position of that green when a BLIND HOLE or SHOT is being played.

Divot   A piece of turf cut out when the club has struck the ball a descending blow. Moderate golfers rarely take a divot. If a slice of turf has been removed it *must* be replaced and tramped down to avoid damage to the course. Not to replace a divot is regarded as an elementary crime.

Dog-leg   For the purpose of variety some golf holes are so constructed that the fairways are not straight. As a rule such holes have an angle which resembles those of a dog's hind legs, sometimes the fairway turns to the left, sometimes to the right. If the hole veers to the left, the hole is called a left-hand dog-leg. If to the right, it is called a right-hand dog-leg. Usually, in the angle, there is a HAZARD of some kind and it takes a brave player, and a good one to try and cut the corner and thus save distance by driving across it.

Dog licence   In match play, when one's opponent is seven holes up and there are only six left to play, the term beaten by a 'dog licence' is used. The seven and six being, in terms of old currency, the price of a dog licence in Britain for many years.

Dormie or dormy   A golfer is deemed to be 'dormie' or 'dormy' if he is as many holes up as there are holes remaining to be played in a MATCH PLAY competition. The same situation applies to a side in the same circumstances. For example, if a golfer is four holes up and four holes remain to be played, he would be 'dormie'. His opponent could not then win the match, but of course he could still halve it by winning the remaining holes. It is incorrect to talk of being 'dormie down'. Chambers Dictionary gives the definitions: 'the player who is "dormie" cannot lose though he goes to sleep'.

Double bogey   The American term for a hole at which the score is two strokes over the PAR score for that hole. (*See also* BOGEY.)

Draw   (1) In a match play competition, there is a draw to decide who plays against whom, or if it is a foursome or four-ball competition, who plays with whom. It is also customary in stroke play competitions for competitors' names to go into a hat to decide who is to play with whom.

(2) The ball is said to be drawn when it is purposely made to fly straight and then pulled to the left for purposes of safety or for setting the ball into a good position for the next stroke.

Drive   To 'drive' the ball is to play the ball from the TEE with a driver. The expression has been used in golf since the early nineteenth century. The expression 'drive' was used in other early sports seven centuries earlier.

'Drive for show, putt for dough'   An American saying, which means that, although driving is more spectacular, the most important part of the game is putting. This idea, held for many years, is not now so popular as it once was.

Driver   The club usually used to hit the ball from the TEEING GROUND. On occasions other clubs are used for reasons of safety or at short holes, well within the range of less powerful clubs.

Drive the green   This means that with one stroke the player has hit the ball from the TEE to the GREEN.

Driving ranges   Driving 'stations', or, in most cases, covered 'bays', where a player wishing to practice can buy or rent a number of balls and bang them off to his heart's content! Some driving ranges have excellent facilities, such as restaurant and refreshment bars, and some also have par 3 courses, which are in effect Pitch and Putt courses. Driving ranges are a recent innovation which originated in the United States. The idea has now spread to many other countries, of these, particularly Japan. There are also many of these ranges in Britain.

Duff *See* FLUFF.

Duffer The expression generally used for a very bad player, more often than not a beginner.

Duck hook An expression which originated in America and which refers to a ball which flies low, then hooks sharply to the left.

Dunlop Masters Tournament An annual 72-hole stroke play tournament sponsored by the Dunlop Organization. It is played annually at selected venues. It was first held in 1946 at Stoneham, Southampton. Entry is restricted to winners of major championships, professional tournaments and invited players.

Dyke An Irish term, which means a hole played in one under PAR.

Eagle A term which originated in America, indicating a score of two under PAR for the hole. It will be noted that the terms describing holes done in under par relate to birds, i.e. birdie: one under par; eagle: two under par; albatross: three under par.

Earliest reference to golf The earliest reference to golf in Britain is contained in the Act of Scottish Parliament, dated March 1457, in which it was decreed that several games and pastimes, including golf, should be banned. The reason for the decree is stated to have been the fact that the citizens were spending too much time with their outdoor sports and not enough in practising archery, this being a necessary exercise in weapon training in those days when wars with the English were common.

Eclectic A competition in which entrants play two or more rounds. The score which counts is the best recorded at each hole for any of the rounds played. The most common method of running this type of competition at most clubs is to make a small charge for each round played. The winner is the player, who when the time limit set for the competition expires has the best eclectic score. For this purpose a player's handicap is taken into account.

Edinburgh Golfers, Honourable Company of One of the most famous clubs in the history of the game. It had its beginnings on the links at Leith, where enthusiasts first gathered to play. The first written evidence of the club's existence appeared in 1744, when the town council of Edinburgh was petitioned by 'several gentlemen of Honour, skillful in the ancient and healthfull exercise of Golf' to donate a silver club to be competed for annually over the links at Leith. The council agreed and the competition was played immediately. Thus was formed the Honourable Company of Edinburgh Golfers, the word 'honourable' being incorporated in the name because, as the petition to the council stated, the golfers were 'gentlemen of Honour'.

A code of rules was drawn up before 1744 and was used for some considerable time. For twenty-four years after its formation the members had no club-house and used a tavern. But in 1768 a club-house was built at a corner of the links and was used until 1831, after which the Honourable Company, having been homeless for five years, settled at Musselburgh in 1836. There they shared a course with two other societies, the Edinburgh Burgess and the Bruntsfield Links. The course, however, became overcrowded and the Honourable Company moved to Muirfield near Gullane in 1891, the site of their present course, which has been the venue of the Open Championship and other famous events on many occasions.

Edward Trophy One of the oldest of golf trophies played annually over 36 holes on the Gailes course of the Glasgow Golf Club. It is played for by amateur golfers and is a SCRATCH competition. Many famous Scottish players have won the trophy.

Eighteen Holes The number of holes in a round of golf. A round, however, has not always comprised 18 holes. For instance, St Andrews and Prestwick originally had 12 holes. There were other courses of fewer holes than that, but eventually St Andrews became 22 holes, 11 out and 11 in. At St Andrews, however, in 1764, the first four holes were made into two and the same thing happened on the inward journey, so that the round then became 18 holes. The practice of 18 holes soon became general and is now the normal number on a golf course, except for those which have little land available. In such instances, the courses are of 9 holes. Some of the early clubs, Blackheath and Leith among them, had only 5 holes, and the first course on Wimbledon Common, that of the London Scottish Club, was composed of 7 holes. Many of the other old clubs had holes of varying numbers. Musselburgh at first had 5, Bruntsfield had 6 and at the other end of the scale, Montrose had 25.

Elysian Fields   A narrow area of the Old Course at St Andrews in Scotland on what might be called the 'uplands', between the 14th tee and Hell bunker.

English Amateur Championship   The youngest of the four home national championships, having begun in 1925. It was first held at the Royal Liverpool Club, Hoylake, the members of which first mooted the idea as they had done many years earlier with the Amateur Championship. The winner in the first two years was T. F. Ellison, a member of the Royal Liverpool Club. Those eligible to play must be English born or have one parent who is English and who was born in England. They must not have competed in the championships of any other of the home countries. In 1957 something of a sensation was caused when a South African, Arthur Walker, won the championship. He was eligible to play since one of his parents was English. Two years later he won the South African Amateur Championship. The English Golf Union, the body of which administers the championship, has the power to admit a golfer with the necessary handicap qualifications (three) and who is a British subject resident in England. It is a match play championship and the venues vary each year.

English Golf Union   Founded in 1924, this is the youngest of the four home unions. At present it controls the golf activities of the county unions, and through them the many golf clubs in England. Its interests include the uniform system of handicapping and arrangements for the English championships.

English Open Amateur Stroke Play Championship   Formerly the Brabazon Trophy, this open medal competition started in 1947. It has been won mostly by English golfers although Ronnie Shade, a Scot and now a professional, won it three times. It is administered by the English Golf Union and is played over 72 holes on a different course each year.

English seaside courses: The first   The first seaside course in England was that of the Royal North Devon Club at Westward Ho! The formation of the club dates back to 1864. Other old clubs in England are the Royal Liverpool Club, at Hoylake, and the Alnmouth Club, at Alnmouth, Northumberland, which were both formed in 1869.

Etiquette   This is an important part of the game and is included in Section 1 of the Rules of Golf, which are as follows:

Courtesy on the Course
   'In the interest of all, players should play without delay.
   'No player should play until the players in front are out of range.
   'Players searching for a ball should signal the players behind them to pass as soon as it becomes apparent that the ball will not easily be found: they should not search for five minutes before doing so.
   'They should not continue play until the players following them have passed and are out of range. When the play of a hole has been completed, players should immediately leave the putting area.'

Behaviour During Play
   'No one should move, talk, or stand close to or directly behind the ball or the hole when a player is ADDRESSING the ball or making a stroke. The player who has the HONOUR should be allowed to play before his opponent or fellow-competitor tees his ball.'

PRIORITY ON THE COURSE

   'In the absence of special rules, two-ball matches should have precedence of and be entitled to pass any three- or four-ball match.
   'A single player has no standing and should give way to a match of any kind.
   'Any match playing a whole round is entitled to pass a match playing a shorter round.

'If a match fails to keep its place on the course and loses more than one clear hole on the players in front, it should allow the match following to pass.'

CARE OF THE COURSE

Holes in Bunkers

'Before leaving a bunker, a player should carefully fill up and smooth over all holes and footprints made by him.'

Restore Divots and Ball-Marks

'THROUGH THE GREEN, a player should ensure that any turf cut or displaced by him is replaced at once and pressed down, and that any damage to the putting green made by the ball or the player is carefully repaired.'

Damage to Greens—Flagsticks, Bags, etc.

'Players should ensure that, when putting down bags, or the flagstick, no damage is done to the putting green, and that neither they nor their caddies damage the hole by standing close to it, in handling the flagstick or in removing the ball from the hole. The flagstick should be properly replaced in the hole before the players leave the putting green.'

Golf Carts

'Local notices regulating the movements of golf carts should be strictly observed.'

Damage through Practice Swings

'In taking practice swings players should avoid causing damage to the course, particularly the tees, by removing DIVOTS.'

European Golf Association Founded in 1937, its members are the unions representing golf clubs in various countries of Europe. It concerns itself only with international golfing affairs, such as championship dates, international matches, and the European Team Championship.

Extra holes played in important competitions The record number of extra holes in any important match play tournament took place at the Walton Heath Golf Club, Surrey, in 1952, when Fred Daly, who went on to win the event, beat Alan Poulton at the 30th or 12th extra hole. In a round of the American Amateur Championship in 1930, at Merion, Pennsylvania, Maurice McCarthy beat George von Elm at the 10th extra hole. These matches are believed to be the longest ever played, certainly as regards important events.

Face (1) The part of the club-head with which the ball is struck. (2) The slope of a bunker or hillock, facing towards the player.

Fade, controlled A shot made with the deliberate intention of bending the ball in flight towards the right. Many of the world's leading professionals have incorporated this style of stroke into their play. A controlled fade can be effected by bringing the face of the club across the ball from right to left at the moment of impact. An uncontrolled fade i.e. a stroke not played deliberately, is a SLICE.

Fairway The cut portion of the course which lies between the teeing grounds and the putting greens. Other ground between the teeing grounds and putting greens is known as the 'ROUGH'. This is the generally accepted idea, but the Rules of Golf take no notice of fairway and rough and merely term the whole ground of a golf course, except the teeing grounds and the putting greens, as being 'through the green'. Generally speaking, however, it is the words 'fairway' and 'rough' which are in common use.

Famous matches Allan Robertson and Tom Morris of St Andrews played the Dunn brothers of Musselburgh for a side-stake said to have been £400. The match was over two rounds and the St Andrews men won by a hole. In the modern era Archie Compston beat Walter Hagen at Moor Park in a 72-hole match by 18 and 17 (18 holes up and 17 to play). In a match at Walton Heath, Henry Cotton and Reg Whitcombe of Britain beat Sid Brews and Bobby Locke of South Africa in a 72-hole match by 2 and 1.

Fastest rounds A South African, Len Richardson, played a round at Mowbray, a course of 6248 yd (5531 m) in 31 minutes 22 seconds. This, according to *The Golfers' Handbook,* is the fastest round played by a golfer on foot.

Fat (1) The 'fat' of the green is an American expression denoting the largest area between the hole and the edge of the green. (2) When in playing an iron, the club-head hits the ground behind the ball, it is said to be hitting a stroke 'fat'.

Feathery or featherie   The type of ball used in the early days of the game. It was composed of a leather skin in which were packed soft boiled feathers. The number required for one ball was equal to the amount which could be fitted into a 'lum hat', a type of headgear popular in the mid 1800s. One of the most famous makers of the feathery golf ball was Allan Robertson of St Andrews. The making of a feathery golf ball, which was done by hand, was an arduous task, and consequently, the price was unbelievably high for that period. The best balls cost as much as five shillings each! Eventually the feathery ball was superseded by the gutta-percha, just before 1850. (*See aslo* GOLF BALL, HISTORY OF.)

Fewest putts   The fewest number of putts recorded in *The Golfers' Handbook* is 14 by Colin Collen-Smith at Betchworth Park, England, during a round in 1947. He had one putt on 14 greens and chipped in from beyond the green four times. In the United States M. D. Chatten had 16 putts at Elkhart, Indiana. He one-putted 14 times, had one two-putt and chipped in three times.

First American woman professional   Miss Helen Hicks, former U.S. Women's champion, became a professional in 1935. She was the forerunner of many American women professionals. Now they have their own tournament circuit.

First British woman professional   After World War II, Miss Poppy Wingate, of Sheffield, competed in a number of professional tournaments as did Miss Meg Farquhar of Lossiemouth. Britain's first tournament professional was Miss Vivien Saunders who in recent years has competed on the U.S. women's professional circuit, as well as in other overseas countries.

First professional   It is generally accepted that Allan Robertson of St Andrews was the first professional.

Flagstick (pin)   The stick or pin with a small flag attached which is placed in the hole on the putting green, thus providing a target for golfers to aim at. The flagstick can be removed in certain circumstances or 'attended' according to the Rules of Golf dealing with the putting green.

Flat   (1) Describes the lie of the club-head in relation to the shaft. (2) A term used to describe a swing when the club is taken back low round the shoulders.

Fluff (duff)   A bad shot. A fluff or duff occurs when the club hits the ground, rather than making solid contact with the ball which either scuttles along the ground a short distance or rises gently in the air.

Follow-through   The movement of the hands and arms after the ball has been hit. After striking the ball the club-head continues on its natural arc, and no effort should be made to restrict it. If the ball has been hit correctly the arms will be at full stretch, and the hands lifted by the momentum of the club-head after it has hit the ball.

Foozle   An expression which describes a bad stroke, not so much in use now as it was formerly. To foozle a shot is to send the ball trundling along the ground.

Fore!   A warning cry to players, or indeed spectators, in a position where they are in danger of being hit by the ball. It is believed that the derivation of 'Fore!' was the term 'Beware before!'

Forecaddie   Forecaddies are not employed nowadays, but were once frequently used by players in such events as the Open Championship to spot the ball immediately it landed. The forecaddie is now banned by the Rules of Golf, but a golfer may send his own caddie forward to spot his ball if he so desires.

Formby   *See* FAMOUS BRITISH CLUBS AND COURSES, p. 146.

Forward press   The movement of the right knee and the hands inwards just before taking the club-head back at the commencement of the shot. The idea is that such a movement generates power to the swing.

Four-ball.   A match in which two players play their better ball against the better ball of their two opponents. The side whose better or scoring ball is holed in fewer strokes than that of their opponents win the hole.

Foursome   A match in which two golfers play against two other golfers, each side playing one ball which is hit by the partners alternately. The side which holes out at a hole in the least number of strokes wins that hole. (*See also* SCOTCH FOURSOMES.)

Freeze   To freeze on a shot means that the player has developed such a state of nerves that he cannot complete the stroke. It usually occurs on the putting green, and is known by other expressions, such as the 'twitch', the 'yips' (Americanism), and the 'jitters'.

Fresh air shot   *See* AIR SHOT.

Front nine   An American expression which refers to the first nine holes of a golf course. Conversely, the second nine is known in America as the back nine.

Frying-pan   An expression used to describe certain types of shot played out of a BUNKER. The frying-pan shot in fact means playing the blaster or wedge underneath the ball with a flat trajectory scooping up a great deal of sand. The result is that the ball lands on the green and stops quickly.

Game, One's   A golfer refers to his game when he describes his form. He is either on his game or not on his game, as the case may be.

Ganton   *See* FAMOUS BRITISH CLUBS AND COURSES, p. 146.

Gate money   The first time gate money was charged in the Open Championship was in 1926 at Royal Lytham and St Annes. So successful was the venture that in the following year the prize money was increased to the then astronomical figure of £275, but gate money had been charged in golf competitions in Britain many years before that. Indeed, it has been said that some of the old timers, when they played their famous money matches, played before spectators, who paid to watch them. Today, gate money is charged at most big tournaments and the Open Championship could not now be the great spectacle that it is without the aid that gate money brings to the funds of the Royal and Ancient Club, the organizers.

'Gimmie'   An Americanism which means that the ball is so close to the hole that it will be conceded by all but the most competitive of opponents.

Glasgow   *See* FAMOUS BRITISH CLUBS AND COURSES, p. 146.

Gleneagles   *See* FAMOUS BRITISH CLUBS AND COURSES, p. 146.

Gloves   Many years ago, golfers, particularly lady golfers, played with gloves. Gradually it was discovered that the fingers of the left-hand glove showed more signs of wear than the right-hand glove. When this was realized, the first golf gloves were made without fingers—the fingers being left free—but now they are complete gloves and the greater percentage of right-handed players today wear a glove on their left hand (the opposite applies to left-handed players).

Gobble   A long putt holed against general expectations, both of the player and the other participants.

'Golden Bear'   The nickname given to Jack Nicklaus the famous American golfer by his admirers early in his career, in view of the fact he had fair hair.

Golf bags   In the first days of golf a player carried his few golf clubs under his arm, or a caddie carried them for him. About 1880 as more clubs came into use rough home-made containers made of canvas became the forerunners of the golf bags, large and small, in use today.

Golf ball, History of   The Romans are said to have played their games with a ball which had a leather cover stuffed with feathers, but there is some indication that the early Scots golfers played with wooden balls and that the 'FEATHERY', as it was called, was not introduced until probably about the middle of the 17th century. By then golf balls were costing much more than they had done fifty years earlier and historians have suggested that the increase in price was due to the wooden ball having given way to its successor. In 1506 golf balls cost only fourpence a dozen and a golf club cost but one penny!

In the early days of the feathery golf ball its manufacture was a monopoly, a man named William Berwick being the sole supplier.

The 'feathery' stayed until the advent of the GUTTY or gutta-percha ball in 1848. Although invented by the Rev. Robert Paterson, the firm of W. T. Henley or a member of their staff is credited with making the first successful gutta-percha ball, which it is said was first played at Blackheath. This ball was used until the end of 19th century when an American, DR COBURN HASKELL, invented the rubber-cored ball.

No size was laid down for the rubber-cored ball and it was not until 1920 that the Royal and Ancient Club decreed that the weight of the ball should not be greater than 1.62 oz (46 g) and the size not less than 1.62 in (41.31 mm) in diameter. In the United States the diameter is 1.68 in (42.82 mm). The bigger ball can be used in international matches in Britain by any player who desires to do so. In the United States it is always used.

In recent years efforts have been made to have a standard-size ball for use throughout the world, but no decision has yet been reached. The size suggested is 1.66 in (42.33 mm).

Golf ball sales   It is estimated that about 20,500,000 golf balls are sold in the British Isles each year and that in the United States the figure is ten times greater. If the rest of the world is taken into account then the sales of golf balls must be in the region of 450,000,000 per year.

Golf book: Earliest   The first golf book published in Great Britain was *The Golfers' Manual* (1857). The author was H. B. Farnie, who wrote his book under the pseudonym 'A Keen Hand'. Many years later, about 1950, a limited and private edition of the book was published. It is remarkable that *The Golfers' Manual* showed so much authority. Some of the points made in it are still true today.

Golf book: The first American   *Golf in America, a practical manual,* was first published in the United States in 1895. The author was James P. Lee.

Golf club, recognized   The definition of a golf club, as approved by the Royal and Ancient Club, is one that regularly appoints office-bearers. From the point of view of the various national unions, a recognized club is one which is affiliated to the Golfers' Union through a county union.

Golf Club Secretaries, Association of   This association was formed with the object of bringing secretaries of golf clubs throughout the country into closer association with each other. The Golf Club Secretaries' Association was formed in 1933.

Golf Development Council   This body was formed in 1965 to co-ordinate the efforts of all bodies concerned with golf. It works closely with the various local and national authorities interested in the game. The founder members were the Royal and Ancient Club, The English, Welsh and Scottish Golf Unions, the Ulster branch of the Golf Union of Ireland, the Ladies' Golf Union, the Professional Golfers' Association, the Golf Foundation, the Artisan Golfers' Association and the National Association of Public Courses.

Golf Foundation The Golf Foundation was formed to encourage boys and girls to take up the game. It is financed by various golf equipment firms, by the proceeds of an annual ball, held in London, and by the proceeds of competitions in which the entry money is donated to the Golf Foundation.

Golf Illustrated Gold Vase One of the oldest amateur golf tournaments dating from 1909. It is played annually over 36 holes and is a scratch competition. Since 1973 the venue has been Walton Heath. Entry is by invitation. Some of the world's greatest amateurs including Harold Hilton, Cyril Tolley, Roger Wethered, Bobby Jones, Joe Carr, Michael Bonallack and John Davies have won the trophy.

Golfing societies No permission from any ruling body is necessary for the formation of societies but many of them become affiliated to the national union of the country. The activities of such societies can vary enormously from the holding of competitions, the playing of matches, or merely semi-social outings. Societies can give their members their own handicaps but such handicaps are only applicable in playing in events held by the society.

Golf library: Biggest The world's biggest golf library is owned by an American enthusiast, Colonel R. Otto Probst, at South Bend, Indiana.

Golf museums The United States Golf Association has a Golf Museum at Golf House, New York, which is their headquarters. There, golf items of all kinds are housed as well as many golf books. At the Royal and Ancient Golf Club at St Andrews, there is a museum of a kind, in which are displayed many old clubs which have been submitted to the club for approval—some are weird indeed! The Royal and Ancient Club also has a fine collection of trophies as do many other of the older golf clubs.

Golf: Origin of the word The name is from the Scottish word 'gouf', meaning to strike or cuff. The original Dutch ball game was sometimes called *kolf,* taking its name from the Dutch word for club. The similarity between the two words would suggest that one of them could have been adapted from the other.

Golf Society of Great Britain. This society was founded by the wealthy Australian, Sir Aynsley Bridgland, who lived in Britain, to foster goodwill in golf nationally and internationally. The association has an arrangement with clubs on whose courses members of the society are allowed to play on favourable terms.

Golf sticks   An archaic term for describing the implements with which the game is played.

Golf trolley   *See* CADDIE CAR.

Golf widow   A lady frequently left alone while her husband plays golf. It is believed that the term was first used in a drawing by Harry Furniss, which depicted a lady gazing out of the window, presumably towards the golf course to which her husband had gone. The illustration was captioned 'A Golf Widow', and appeared in the Badminton Library on Golf which was published in 1890.

Golf Writers' Trophy   Awarded annually by the British Association of Golf Writers to the man, woman or team who has, in their opinion, done most for British golf in that year. It was inaugurated in 1951.

Goose-necked putter (wry-necked)   A putter made with a curve in the neck, so that the shaft is joined nearer to the centre of the head of the putter. Once fashionable but not so much now since the introduction of centre-shafted putters.

Grain   This refers to the way in which the grass has been cut. On the putting surface every alternate line is different, each line being the width of the cutter blade of the mower. When the grass is cut, the roller smooths the blades in one direction. Grain is not so pronounced in Britain as in other countries where the grass on the greens is of a somewhat coarser variety. (*See also* NAP.)

Grass bunkers   Grassy hollows which can still be found on some golf courses, and which do service as HAZARDS!

Great Triumvirate, The   *See* TRIUMVIRATE, THE GREAT.

Green   In the early days of golf the word green was used to describe the whole area of a course and the term 'through the green', still used in the Rules of Golf, is derived from the original meaning. 'Green' now refers to the surface of the ground prepared for putting.

Green fee   The amount payable if a visitor wants to play a round at a private golf club. Green fee charges vary as do the conditions of play. Some clubs insist on a visitor producing a letter of introduction from the secretary of his own club. Others insist that all visitors must be accompanied by a member of the club.

Green, Through the   (1) In terms of the Rules, this means the whole area of the course except the teeing ground and the putting surface of the hole being played, as well as all hazards on the course. The original meaning of the word 'green' which now refers to the putting area, still survives in description, such as 'Greenkeeper', the person responsible for keeping the course in order, and also in the 'Green Committee' of a golf club, the committee which supervises the condition of the greens of a golf course and policies relating to the upkeep of the course.

(2) An expression used to describe a ball that has landed either short or on the putting surface and has run over to the area at the back of the green.

Greensome   A type of FOUR-BALL match, unofficial, in which all four players drive, and then each side selects the ball with which they wish to continue to complete the hole. As a matter of custom, the longer drive is usually chosen, but not necessarily so; it may be that one player has put his ball in the rough and his partner is an expert at recovery shots. In that case he would play the second shot.

Grip   (1) Describes the way the golf club is held. In some respects it is an incorrect expression, the word 'grip' having the meaning 'to grasp firmly' and grasping a golf club too firmly is not in the best interest of the player. (2) Grip can also mean that part of the shaft at the top of the club which is covered in leather or a plastic material.

Grips, Types of   The most popular method of holding a golf club is by the 'overlapping grip'. This was said to have been invented by the great Harry Vardon and certainly it was popularized by him, although his contemporary, J. H. Taylor, claims he first used this grip. The Vardon Grip, as it is generally known, is one in which the little finger of the right hand overlaps the index finger of the left hand. Another type of grip is the 'interlocking grip' in which the little finger of the right hand interlocks with the index finger of the left hand. The third type of grip is the 'two-handed grip', in which both hands hold the club separately. There is no contact between the hands except that they both press together. Many golfers have their own variation of the grip, but basically, the three mentioned above are the ones in general use. The grips described are, of course, only applicable to right-handed players. There are a few golfers, all of them self-taught, who grip the club with the left hand below the right and who hit the ball in a right-handed manner. It is an established fact that if one gives a child a golf club to hold, he or she will invariably have their left hand below the right hand. For putting, which is a very individual part of the game, golfers have their own methods of gripping the putter and although many players have claimed from time to time to have discovered the secret of putting, by holding the putter in one way or another, there are no hard and fast rules.

Grooved swing   This expression emanated in the United States. It is used to describe a swing during which the clubhead moves along the same imaginary path each time a stroke is played.

Ground score   Two golf clubs in Britain, Elie and Coventry, claim to have been the first to have given each hole on their respective courses a figure which represented the score which a scratch golfer might be expected to achieve. This was towards the end of 1890.

Ground the club   To 'ground the club' is to place the clubhead on the ground behind the ball, before making a stroke. It is not permissible to ground the club in a HAZARD, such as a BUNKER.

Gullane   *See* FAMOUS BRITISH CLUBS AND COURSES, p. 146.

Gutty ball   The gutty or gutta ball was first made in 1848 by the Rev. Robert Paterson, who conceived the idea after seeing gutta-percha packing round a statue 'Vishnu' which is now in St Andrews University. The ball was called the 'Paterson Patent' but was not a success because it had a smooth cover and flew badly. Golfers using the gutta discovered that they flew better after they had been damaged by blows from clubs, so soon they

South African Gary Player has won every major championship, including the British Open Championship (three times), the U.S. Open Championship and the U.S. Masters. Here he is playing out of a bunker during the Piccadilly Match Play Championship at Wentworth, of which he has been a frequent winner

(*above*) Lee Trevino who in 1971 won the U.S. Open Championship, the British Open Championship and the Canadian Open Championship in the space of four weeks. Trevino is one of the world's most colourful golfers. (*below*) The Scot Bernard Gallacher has scored several big successes, his biggest to date being the Dunlop masters in 1974

Brian Barnes, another Scots professional, although he has lived all his life in England. Like Gallacher he has played for Great Britain and Scotland. He is the 1975 French Open Champion

were scoring the covers with a chisel. The first successful gutty ball was made and marketed by the firm of W. T. Henley.

Halford Hewitt Challenge Cup   A competition for old boys of public schools, it was originated in 1924 by Mr Halford Hewitt, a keen public-school golfer. It is said to be the world's largest tournament, with players coming in teams of ten from 64 public schools. The competition is played by foursomes, those matches finishing level at the 18th hole counting as a half. The competition is always played at the Royal Cinque Ports Club, Deal, with earlier rounds also at neighbouring Royal St George's, Sandwich.

Half shot   Now virtually unknown in golf, but in the early days of the game when players carried fewer golf clubs, they had to improvise to a great degree, so that if they used a long-iron shot but the distance to the green was not such as to justify it, they played a 'half shot'.

Halving a hole   A hole is halved when each side has HOLED OUT in the same number of strokes and a game is halved when each side finishes level by winning the same number of holes in match play. In stroke play, a half would mean that the opposing players had taken the same number of strokes. A player receiving a stroke at a hole on handicap would achieve a half by scoring a five to his opponent's four.

Handicaps   No golfer can enter a competition without first having had a handicap allotted by his club. Before starting in a competition the player is responsible for seeing that he is playing under the correct handicap. In the case of match play or bogey competitions he is responsible for seeing that strokes are given or taken at the correct holes. If a player plays off a higher handicap than his current one he will be disqualified. If he plays off a lower handicap, the score or the result of the match will stand.

Hanging lie   Describes the ball when it is lying on a downward slope and usually resting on a tuft of grass.

Haskell (rubber-cored) ball   The ball in general use by golfers. It is constructed by winding strips of elastic round a metal or liquid-filled core, the casing being of gutta-percha or an artificial compound. This rubber-cored ball superseded the gutty ball. Its inventor was Dr Coburn Haskell, of Cleveland, Ohio. The first big win with the Haskell, or rubber-cored ball, was in the U.S. Amateur Championship in 1901. So far as Britain is concerned, the first big success with the Haskell ball was Sandy Herd's victory in the Open Championship in 1902.

Hazards   Obstructions in the way of a golf shot. Hazards are clearly defined in the Rules of Golf. BUNKERS are a hazard, so is a stream or pond. (Bare patches of ground, roads, paths across golf courses and the like are not hazards.) To be more precise, a bunker is an area of bare ground, but almost always a depression covered with sand.

A water hazard is any pond, river, ditch, surface drainage, or any other water source. Theoretically one can play from a water hazard, but for obvious reasons this is not often possible. If, however, the ball is in mud or in shallow water, golfers do risk playing the ball and there are on record some famous golf strokes so executed.

A lateral water hazard is a water hazard of the kind described above, which runs approximately parallel to the line of play, so that it is not possible to drop the ball behind it and keep to the spot at which the ball last crossed the hazard, between the player and the hole. Hazards are frequently altered on courses by the committee of golf clubs or officials running tournaments. When that is done, the extent of the hazards should be accurately defined.

Head up   Raising the head when playing a stroke with the result that the eyes are taken off the ball is thought by many to be the most common fault in playing golf. Unless the eye is kept on the ball, it is obviously difficult to hit an accurate shot.

Hickory   Before the advent of steel shafts, made legal in 1929, most shafts were of hickory wood.

Highest golf club in Europe   Said to be the course at Sestrière, near Turin in Northern Italy, which is over 6500 ft (1900 m) above sea level.

Highest golf course in the world   The highest golf course in the world is claimed by Bolivia, in South America. This is at La Paz, the capital, where the height of the club above sea level is 13,500 ft (4115 m).

Highest score at one hole   In a major event, 26, by Tommy Armour at the 17th hole in the Shawnee Tournament in 1927. In the first Open Championship at Prestwick a competitor whose name is not in the records took 21 at one hole. In the 1950 Open Championship at Troon a well-known German amateur, Herman Tissies, took 15 at the short 8th hole. He finished with a creditable 92.

Hockey at the halt (Or 'ockey at the 'alt.)   A derisory description of golf. The expression is said to have emanated from the utterance of an army Sergeant-major some time at the end of last century.

Hole   (1) On every green, the ultimate target for every golfer. It is $4\frac{1}{4}$ in (10.8 cm) in diameter and at least 4 in (10.2 cm) deep. The lining, which is used to keep the ground from crumbling, should be sunk at least 1 in (2.5 cm) below the putting surface. (2) Hole can also mean the entire playing area between tee and green.

Hole-in-one   When a player hits the ball from the tee and it finishes in the hole on the green, he is said to have done a hole-in-one. The American term is an 'ace' and the expression is gaining some ground in this country. Many instances arise every year of golfers HOLING OUT in one.

Hole-in-one: First recorded   Young Tom Morris, when he won his first Open Championship in Prestwick in 1868, HOLED OUT in one at the 8th hole.

Hole-in-one: Greatest number   The American professional, Art Wall, claims to have achieved 37 holes-in-one in his career. He was a well-known American tournament player and played against Britain in the Ryder Cup three times. Charles T. Chevalier, who was for many years professional at the Heaton Moor Club in Lancashire, has 30 holes-in-one to his credit.

Hole-in-one: Longest   The longest hole-in-one is said to have been accomplished by an American named Bob Mitera, at the Miracle Hill Club in Omaha, in 1965. There was a strong following wind and the hole, the 10th hole on the course, was downhill. It measured 444 yd (406 m). The longest hole-in-one in Britain is a 380 yd (347 m) hit in 1961 by David Hulley. The hole was the 5th at Tankersley Park, Sheffield, Yorkshire. These and other records are included in *The Golfers' Handbook*.

Holes-in-one: Important events   In the final of the Irish Open Amateur Championship at Royal County Down in 1933, Eric Fiddian had two holes-in-one against his opponent, Jack McLean. McLean won the final by 3 and 2 (3 holes up and 2 to play).

In 1971 in the Martini Professional Tournament at Royal Norwich, John Hudson from the Hendon Club, Middlesex, HOLED OUT in one at two successive holes (11th and 12th), in the second round.

Holes-in-one: Most in a year   11 by Mr J. Boydstone, an American golfer. He achieved the feat in 1962.

Holes-in-one: Oldest player   C. Youngman HOLED OUT in one in 1971 at the Tam O'Shanter Club in Toronto at the age of 93.

Holes-in-one: Youngest player   Tommy Moore, aged 6 years and 1 month, HOLED OUT in one at Woodbrier, West Virginia in 1968.

Holing out (Holed out)   To hit the ball into the hole.

Holes up   The extent of a victory over an opponent in match play when the match has been continued for the full number of holes specified. This form of calculating the results of match play is not used much today, although it was popular mainly in team events some years ago. Suggestions have been made that the system should be revived in such events as the Oxford versus Cambridge University annual match.

Home green   The 9th green of a nine-hole course or the 18th green of an 18-hole course.

Home internationals   The series of internationals for men and women played annually between England, Ireland, Scotland and Wales. The men's matches began in 1932 at Troon. The women's in 1948 at Royal Lytham.

Honour   To take the honour is to play first from the teeing ground. The question as to who takes the honour on the first tee can be decided by lot, i.e. tossing for it in the usual manner. If there has been a draw for a competition, the players (or player) whose names appear higher on the draw-list play first.

Honourable Company of Edinburgh Golfers   *See* EDINBURGH GOLFERS, HONOURABLE COMPANY OF.

Hood *See* CLUB-HEAD COVERS OR HOODS.

Hooding the club When the loft of the club is decreased by having the ball nearer the right foot at address than it would be for a normal shot, and closing the face of the club by pressing the hands forward towards the line of flight of the ball. (*See also* SHUTTING THE FACE.)

Hook The ball is said to be hooked when it veers viciously to the left from its intended line of flight. There can be several reasons for a hook, one of the more usual ones being a swing at the ball too quickly with a flat swing, i.e. a swing in which the club-head is taken round the shoulders.

Hunstanton *See* FAMOUS BRITISH CLUBS AND COURSES, p. 147.

Hustler *See* BANDIT.

Identification Making certain that the ball about to be hit is that belonging to the golfer who is playing the shot. On no account must the ball be lifted for the purpose of identification, except in certain instances, when it is not possible to identify it in any other way.

Illegal clubs Clubs, the implements with which golf is played, must be of a recognized pattern. Any clubs of which the maker or inventor is doubtful must be submitted to the Royal and Ancient Club for approval if it is desired that the clubs are to be used generally, or to the United States Golf Association if the clubs are to be used only in the United States. The two governing bodies keep in close contact with each other over such matters. (*See also* REJECTED CLUBS.)

Impact The moment when the club-head makes contact with the ball.

In contention An expression now becoming more general in golf. It describes the situation when a golfer or golfers have a reasonable chance of winning a tournament during the progress of the event.

Inns as club-houses Before the days of club-houses, players frequently went to a nearby tavern after a game. Several instances still exist of golf clubs having their headquarters at an inn. One such club is the Bramshaw Club, in Hampshire, England, where the club-house is part of The Bell Inn.

Inside to out   The golf swing is on various planes and 'inside to out' is the expression used to describe the action of the club-head in as much as it is taken back and upwards inside the line of flight and finishes with the club-head travelling to the right of the line of flight, that is outside the line of flight. The result is that the ball flies from the right to the left of the line of flight. It is the reverse of OUTSIDE TO IN.

Inverness   *See* FAMOUS AMERICAN CLUBS, p. 154.

Ireland, Golfing Union of   The oldest of the four national unions. It was founded in 1891.

Irish Amateur Championship   Inaugurated in 1893 and open to male amateur golfers of Irish birth or those who have one parent who is Irish. For the purposes of golf, as for some other sports, Ireland is regarded as being one country. It is a match play championship and the venues vary.

Irons   Clubs with iron heads have been used since the game was first played. In the early days they were known in the main as 'cleeks'. It is said there were only three types at the start but the Scots soon enlarged the number. Nowadays, instead of 'driving irons', 'mashie irons', and the like, iron clubs are graded, usually from 2 to 9, but there are other computations. It seems a pity that romantic names such as 'mashie iron', 'lofting iron', 'driving iron', 'driving cleek' have gone out of fashion. Now iron clubs are merely numbers. (*See also* THE IMPLEMENTS OF THE GAME, p. 24.)

Jaggies   An old Scots expression to describe deep ROUGH. Jaggies is another Scots term for nettles which grow in profusion in Scotland even on some golf courses.

Jerk   The quick raising of the shoulders which causes head movement and the subsequent topping of the ball.

Jersey   Jersey and indeed other Channel Islands as well have a special place in the world of golf because some of the finest golfers have hailed either from Jersey or Guernsey. Harry Vardon and his brothers, the great Ted Ray, the Boomers, the Gaudins, the Stickleys, Charles Chevalier, all came from the Channel Islands. The present-day tournament professional, Tommy Horton, is also a Channel Islander, as is the young woman golfer, Carol Le Feuvre. (Mrs R. Gibbs.)

Jigger An iron club with a thin face, greatly favoured by golfers of bygone days. It was used mainly for hitting the ball out of the ROUGH and for long shots from a bare LIE.

Jitters A popular expression used to describe a player who is in a state of nerves, usually associated with his temperament on the putting green.

Jump When the ball bounds over a BUNKER or HAZARD it is said to have 'jumped' it.

Jungle (tiger) country Refers to very heavy ROUGH in that part of a golf course where, to the golfers' imagination at least, the ROUGH appears like a jungle.

Knock-out competition A popular expression used in most golf clubs to describe a match play competition in which the players are drawn against each other with the winner going forward to the next round. It can apply equally to singles or pairs.

Kolbe, kolf, kolven The words *kolbe* and *kolf* are Dutch words which mean club. *Kolven* was the name of a game played in the 16th century in Holland (or what was then referred to as the Low Countries) and claimed by some to be the forerunner of golf. (*See also* HISTORY OF GOLF, p. 9.)

Ladies' clubs: Oldest The oldest ladies' golf club in the world is the St Andrews Ladies' Club whose history dates back to 1867. The Westward Ho! Ladies' Club was formed the following year. There is evidence, however, that ladies played golf at Musselburgh long before that, and that they held competitions for prizes given by male golfers.

Ladies' Golf: First champion The first winner of the Ladies' Championship which was played at Lytham and St Anne's, Lancashire, in 1893, was Lady Margaret Scott, who beat Miss Pearson. Lady Margaret then proceeded to win the title for the next two years. (*See also* BRITISH LADIES' AMATEUR CHAMPIONSHIP.)

Ladies' Golf Union This body was formed in 1893 mainly through the enthusiasm of Miss Isette Pearson of the Royal Wimbledon Club. Miss Pearson was the first secretary. Its authority is recognized in most parts of the world. It promotes the interests of golf as far as women are concerned, and its rules are those under which women's golf is played. It has its own handicapping system and it organizes the British Ladies' Championship and international fixtures. The Ladies' Golf Union works in conjunction with the Royal and Ancient Golf Club and with various organizations overseas. (*See also* HISTORY OF GOLF, p. 15.)

Ladies' tee The teeing ground used by lady golfers. The ladies' tee is usually, but not always, in front of the men's tee. The ladies' PAR of the course is calculated in distances from the ladies' tees, and the handicapping arranged accordingly.

Lady Golfer, First It is on record that the ill-fated Mary Queen of Scots played golf. History records that she indulged in the game shortly after the death of her husband Darnley in 1567. (*See* HISTORY OF GOLF, p. 12.)

Lag-up An American term meaning that a player has, from some considerable distance, put the ball close to the hole. Usually the term is used when it appears that the player, rather than go all out for the hole, has played for safety.

Lateral water hazard *See* HAZARDS.

Left hand below right Sometimes referred to as 'cack-handed' (left-handed). The few golfers who play with the left hand below the right, are invariably those who have never had any lessons. A child given a golf club to hold will almost certainly place the left hand below the right. The most famous golfer who uses this style is the coloured South African, Sewsunker Sewgolum, who achieved a fair measure of success with it, including winning the Dutch Open Championship three times. A famous Belgian Amateur between the wars, Joseph Charles, also used this style and with it won the Belgian Open Amateur Championship and the Luxembourg Open Amateur Championship twice.

Left-handed golfers As in other sports, golf has its quota of left-handed golfers, the most famous being the New Zealander, Bob Charles, who won the Open Championship in 1963 at Royal Lytham. He is one of the world's leading professionals. The most famous British left-hander is P. B. ('Laddie') Lucas who played for Britain in three Walker Cup matches. Miss

Kathryn Phillips, who won the British Girls' Championship in 1968, is also a left-hander.

Leith Links   It is believed that golf was first played on the links at Leith. Certainly Leith has many early associations with the game. The first club there was formed in 1768 when the Company of Edinburgh Golfers banded to form a club. The Edinburgh Burgess Club, now the Royal Burgess Golfing Society of Edinburgh, also played at Leith Links. Both clubs later moved to different locations, the Company of Edinburgh Golfers, now the Honourable Company of Edinburgh Golfers, eventually to take up residence at their present home at Muirfield. (*See also* EDINBURGH GOLFERS, HONOURABLE COMPANY OF.)

Lie (of the ball)   Where the ball comes to rest after being played is the 'lie' of the ball. The ball must be played from that lie unless it is intended to obtain relief as in the case of an unplayable lie. There are various types of lies: bad lies, good lies, hanging lies, downhill lies, uphill lies, tight or close lies, which are all self-explanatory.

Lift and drop   When the ball has to be lifted because it is not possible to play it from the position in which it lies, it may be dropped in the manner prescribed by the Rules of Golf. (*See* BALL DROPPED.) Usually there is a penalty for lifting and dropping but not always. A close scrutiny of the rules should be made.

Lightning   The Rules of Golf (Rule 37, 6) entitle a golfer to discontinue play in a competition without penalty if he or she considers there is danger from lightning. Standing under trees during a lightning thunderstorm is dangerous. Umbrellas are also dangerous during a lightning storm, as are golf clubs. There have been a number of deaths from lightning on golf courses, including that of the Scottish international football player, John White, who was killed on the Crews Hill course, England, on 21 July 1964. Three golfers were killed by lightning on a golf course at Scranton, Penn, in 1957.

Like as we lie   A term used to indicate that each golfer has played the same number of strokes at a given hole.

Like, Playing the   To play a stroke which will put you level with your opponent or partner in the matter of scores at a given hole.

84

Line (of the hole)   The shortest, or, in some cases, the best and safest line which the ball should follow after it is hit.

Links   Ground on which golf is played, mostly descriptive of seaside courses. The word 'links' is a Scottish and northern term meaning gently undulating, sandy ground with coarse grass near the seashore.

Lip (of the hole)   The edge of the hole. A term used when the ball finishes on the brink.

Little Aston   *See* FAMOUS BRITISH CLUBS AND COURSES, p. 147.

Local knowledge   A golfer familiar with a course and adept at putting his experience of it to good use, is said to possess local knowledge. In friendly games a visitor sometimes tries (without much success as a rule) to obtain an extra stroke or two from his opponent to off-set the home man's 'local knowledge'.

Local rules   All golf clubs have rules relating to certain points on their particular course. These arise through factors not present on other courses.

Loft the ball, To   To play the ball high over some object or HAZARD, natural or man-made. It is usually a shot played near the green.

Longest championship final match   Forty-first hole in the 1966 United States Ladies' Championship at Pittsburgh. Mrs Carner (Jo Anne Gunderson) beat Mrs J. D. Streit (Miss Marlene Stewart). The longest championship matches played in the British Isles were in the Irish Amateur Close Championship in 1952 at the Royal Belfast where Tom Egan beat J. C. Brown at the 41st hole, and in the 1960 English Amateur Championship at Hunstanton where Douglas Sewell beat Martin Christmas also at the 41st hole.

Longest championship golf course   In 1968 Carnoustie was extended to 7252 yd (6531 m) with a PAR of 72. The stretching was achieved by means of building new tees further back from the original sites.

Longest drives   In 1934 T. H. Haydon, a member of the Royal Wimbledon Club playing at Budleigh Salterton, Devon, drove the ball 456 yd (417 m) at the 9th green. The hole was downhill.
      The longest drive in a British Open Championship was that of

Craig Wood at St Andrews in 1933. At the 5th hole with a following wind Wood reached a bunker 430 yd (393 m) from the tee. In his play-off with Doug Sanders in the 1970 Open Championship at St Andrews, Jack Nicklaus drove over the 18th green, his tee-shot being estimated at 380 yd (347.5 m).

In 1892 Edward Blackwell drove from the last tee at St Andrews to the club-house steps, a distance of 366 yd (335 m). This was an astounding performance, having in mind the equipment of that time.

Longest hole At the Black Mountain Club in California there is reputed to be a hole of 745 yd (681 m). As regards championship courses the 16th at the Olympic Country Club at San Francisco is 614 yd (561.4 m). In Britain the 6th at Troon, scene of the 1973 British Open Championship, is 580 yd (530 m).

Loop (1) Describes the movement of the club-head at the top of the swing which destroys any chance of it being brought down on the same plane. The most famous exponent of a loop at the top of the swing was the late Jimmy Bruen, the Irish amateur golfer. The effect of a loop is to put the club-head out of its groove, but Bruen was successful in bringing the club-head back into its true path just before impact with the ball. (2) A sequence of golf holes which begin at one point of a course and return to the same point or near the same point. Perhaps the most famous example is at the Old Course, St Andrews, where the 8th, 9th, 10th and 11th holes form a loop.

Loose impediments Objects which are not growing, such as stones or twigs. These may be removed, without, of course, moving the ball.

Lost ball When a golf ball cannot at once be traced after it has been played, players are permitted five minutes to search for it. If after that time the ball has not been found it is deemed to be lost and another must be played as laid down by the Rules of Golf.

Lowest nine holes This record (in a major event, at least) is held by Tony Jacklin when in 1970 he played the first nine holes at St Andrews in 29. Play had to be stopped because of a storm and Jacklin completed his round next day in 67.

Low scoring Low-scoring feats are difficult to assess due to some courses being shorter and easier than others, but in major events, the lowest championship score would seem to be that of Baldovina Dassu, a young Italian professional at Crans in the 1971 Swiss Championship. He recorded a round of 60 on a course of 6885 yd (6295 m).

At Worthing in 1952 Tom Haliburton returned a 61 and followed with a round of 65, giving him 126 for 36 holes, a feat achieved in the United States by Johnny Palmer, Tommy Bolt, Sam Snead and Chandler Harper.

The American star, Johnny Miller, scored 61 over a 7300 yd (6675 m) course at Tucson in January 1975. The British professional, Peter Butler, played a round of 61 over the Old Course at Sunningdale in the Bowmaker Tournament in 1967. Doug Sewell, a British professional, carded a 60 in a minor competition at Ferndown, England.

Lucifer Golfing Society   This society formed in 1921 has a membership limited to 100. It was to be known as the Match Society but on discovering there was already a society of that name, Lucifer instead of Match was decided on. Its chief fixture now is the annual Lucifer Empire meeting for overseas golfers, played each year at Walton Heath in England with qualifying rounds on selected courses.

Make a four   The term used when three golfers invite another to join them so that they may engage in a foursome or a four-ball game.

Marker   (1) A person who goes round with competitors to record the score. (2) A small object used to denote the spot from which a ball has been lifted on the green.

Mashie   A famous club much used in former years. Now golf clubs except the driver, the WEDGE, the BLASTER and the putter are all numbered. The modern No 5 iron corresponds to the mashie. The word mashie took its name from the fact that when used by bad (or unlucky) golfers it cut or 'mashed' the ball.

Mashie niblick   An old club which has been replaced by the modern No 7 iron. The mashie niblick had a more lofted face than a mashie and was in fact halfway to a NIBLICK. Hence the name.

Master Golfer   The unofficial title given to any winner of the Masters Tournament (U.S.) or the Dunlop Masters Tournament.

Masters Tournament This famous American Tournament is played each year at the Augusta National Club. The National course was the brainchild of the late R. T. Jones, one of the greatest golfers in the history of the game. The first Masters Tournament was played in 1934, the winner being the great American golfer, Horton Smith. The Masters is not an open event but is by invitation. Among the rewards for winning the event is a ceremonial green blazer or jacket. (For winners *see* p. 188.)

Matched set A number of golf clubs, usually fourteen, which are graded and numbered. (*See* SET:IRONS.)

Matches: Various kinds Recognized golf matches come into six categories. Single, when one golfer plays another; threesome, when three players go out together and one plays the better ball of the other two; foursome, when four players go out and two play against two, each side using one ball; three-ball, when three players go out and each plays against the others, each using his own ball; better ball, when one player plays the better ball of either two or three players; four-ball, when two players on the one side play the better ball of the two players on the other side. There are other types of matches such as a greensome, where four players (one pair playing against the other) go out together and all drive off the tee. Thereafter they can nominate which of the two drives is to be played for the rest of the hole. Variations of this theme are sometimes used for friendly games, one being when a side nominates which ball of the opposing side is to be played.

Match play A match in which the outcome is decided by holes won.

Medal play *See* STROKE PLAY.

Medal tee The tee or part of a tee, usually further back than normal, off which competitors in a competition are expected to play.

Merion *See* FAMOUS AMERICAN GOLF CLUBS, p. 154.

Merry An expression meaning that the ball has gone past the hole. Usually it describes a putt but can also be used to describe an approach shot.

Minikahda *See* FAMOUS AMERICAN GOLF CLUBS, p. 154.

Mixed foursomes competitions   There are a number of important mixed foursomes competitions. These competitions are also a feature of club golf.

Montrose   *See* FAMOUS BRITISH CLUBS AND COURSES, p. 147.

Moortown   *See* FAMOUS BRITISH CLUBS AND COURSES, p. 147.

Mosely Hurst   Old histories suggest that golf was played at Mosely Hurst near London in the middle of the 18th century, about the same time that golf, or a game resembling it, was said to have been played at Westminster.

Most holes played in 24 hours   Peter Chambers, at Scarborough and South Cliff Golf Club, England, in 1971, Bruce Sutherland at Craiglockhart, Scotland, in 1927, and Stan Gard at North Brighton, Australia, in 1938, all completed 14 rounds. Chambers actually played 14 rounds plus 5 holes, making 257 holes. Gard played 14 rounds and 4 holes, making 256 holes. Sutherland's performance covered 14 rounds exactly.

Muff   To muff a shot is to fluff it or, to be more precise, to make a mess of it.

Muirfield   *See* FAMOUS BRITISH CLUBS AND COURSES, p. 147.

Mulligan   An American expression not used in Britain. In friendly games in the United States a golfer gives a 'Mulligan' when he grants a second chance to his opponent if the opponent has had a bad drive. The term 'bad drive' in this concept means a drive after which the ball has gone only a few yards or in fact the ball has been missed altogether.

Municipal Golf Courses   *See* PUBLIC GOLF COURSES.

Musselburgh   The old town near Edinburgh has an honoured place in golf, and the original Musselburgh club dates back to 1774. There is still a golf course on the original site at Musselburgh, which is now surrounded by the Musselburgh racecourse. The Musselburgh Club, now the Royal Musselburgh Club, has a new home. The Honourable Company of Edinburgh Golfers and the Royal Burgess Club also had their home on the Musselburgh Links at one time. (*See also* HISTORY OF GOLF, p. 12.)

Nap   The cut surface of the green. Grass lies according to the

89

direction in which it has been mowed. The resultant nap is not so prominent in Britain as overseas where the grass is coarser. When the ball moves with the lie of the grass it goes faster than against the nap. So a close examination of the green is necessary to judge the strength of a putt. (See also GRAIN.)

Nassau A favourite variation, adding spice to the game, in the United States. A player winning the first nine holes is awarded a point, and the winner of the entire 18 holes gains another point.

Never up, never in An expression used to describe a putt struck so weakly that the ball stops short of the hole.

Newport See FAMOUS AMERICAN CLUBS, p. 154.

Niblick The old name for a deep-faced club used for hitting the ball out of BUNKERS or long grass. Also used for LOFTING over a HAZARD. The old niblicks had small deep faces unlike their modern counterparts, the No 10 iron, the WEDGE or BLASTER.

Nine-hole course Usually such courses have two different teeing grounds at each hole, one set being used first time round, and the second set being used if players want to complete 18 holes. There are many such golf courses.

Northerly course, Most The most northerly course in the world is in northern Sweden inside the Arctic Circle at Björkliden. It has become a favourite haunt for enthusiasts, often Scots who, not content with being able to play almost all night in the north of their own country, make regular pilgrimages to Björkliden to play by the light of the midnight sun.

Oakland Hills See FAMOUS AMERICAN CLUBS, p. 155.

Oakmont See FAMOUS AMERICAN CLUBS, p. 155.

Observer At international golf matches, such as the Ryder Cup between professionals of the British Isles and the United States, an observer goes out with each match to advise the referee if a ruling is required on any difficult situation that may arise.

Odd, Playing the To play a stroke which will make a player one more than his opponent. Conversely, 'playing the like' means he will, after he has played his stroke, be level with his opponent.

Oldest British amateur champion   The Hon Michael Scott won the British Amateur Championship when 54 in 1933. He continued to play good golf for many years. The oldest American amateur champion was Jack Westland who won the title at 47 in 1952 at Seattle.

Oldest British Open champion   *See* BRITISH OPEN CHAMPIONSHIP, OLDEST WINNERS.

Oldest golf clubs   Scotland: The Honourable Company of Edinburgh Golfers 1744; England: Royal Blackheath 1787; India: Royal Calcutta 1829; Mauritius: Mauritius Naval and Military Club 1844; France: Golf Club de Pau 1856; New Zealand: Otago Golf Club 1856; Canada: Royal Montreal 1873; Ireland: Royal Belfast 1881; Ceylon (Sri Lanka): Royal Colombo Club 1882; Wales: Borth and Ynyslas 1885; Belgium: Royal Antwerp 1888; United States: St Andrews Club 1888; Hong Kong: Royal Hong Kong 1889; Australia: Royal Melbourne 1891.

Oldest golfer   There have been recorded instances of a golfer playing at the age of 100. Several years ago a member of the Hampstead Club in London celebrated his 100th birthday by playing several rounds on the putting green. There was also the instance of a St Andrews clergyman of 90 being given free golf for life on local courses. He lived for several years to take advantage of the offer. Many golfers play well into their nineties.

Oldest U.S. Open champion   Ted Ray, the British golfer, who won the championship at Toledo, Ohio, when he was 43.

Old Man Par   An expression meaning PAR for the course.

Olympic   *See* FAMOUS AMERICAN CLUBS, p. 155.

One-armed Championship   An annual championship in Britain for golfers who play one-handed and are barred from using any artificial aids. A similar competition exists in the United States.

Open Stance   The position at ADDRESS when the left foot is drawn back from the intended line of flight. It is the opposite of CLOSED STANCE. With an open stance if the ball is hit correctly it will fly to the left of the target. Some golfers use an open stance because they have a tendency to play the ball to the right. Others use it so as to fade the ball to the right intentionally.

Open to shut   When the wrists are turned to the right on the backswing and rolled over to the left on the downward swing. The effect is to smother the ball which will scuttle along the ground towards the left.

Open up the hole   Most golf greens are guarded by bunkers, so it is prudent to choose a route to the hole which avoids such hazards. The aim therefore should be to play the approach shot to the green from a position which will afford a margin of safety. Such an approach can only be played if the previous shot has been well planned.

Out of bounds   The boundary beyond which the ball cannot be played. An artificial boundary can be created by officials of a club to ensure that a wayward shot is penalized. In the early days players could hit the ball from any position, even off the course. On some courses to this day a golfer can play his ball from a beach because there is no fence marking the boundary of the course.

Outside agency   According to the Rules of Golf an outside agency is in effect any agency, i.e. animal, bird or man, which is not part of a golf match.

Outside to in   Describes the action of the club-head when it is taken back outside the line of flight and so finishes to the left of the ball before straightening out just before impact. The result is that the ball swings from left to right in flight. 'Inside to out' is the reverse.

Over the green   Describes a shot hit too strongly so that the ball finishes beyond the putting surface.

Oxford and Cambridge Golfing Society   This society for Oxford and Cambridge golfers past and present was suggested by a famous Cambridge golfer, John Low. The 'Society', as it is generally called, was formed on 23rd March 1898. Each year it organizes the President's Putter, which began in 1920.

Oxford and Cambridge match   This annual match between the two universities was first played in 1887.

Paganica One of the oldest known games, played by hitting a ball or some round object with a stick or implement. The Romans, it is said, played this game. (*See also* HISTORY OF GOLF, p. 9.)

Pall Mall or pell mell An early ball game which originated in France. The essentials were a wooden ball and a mallet, although another form was played with a large iron hoop at the end of a pole and the ball resembled a cannon-ball. The object was to hold the ball in the hoop and deposit it in a large hole. The rules are obscure. This game was played at the Freemason's Arms in Hampstead, London, only a few years ago. Pall Mall was played on an enclosed space unlike some of the other Continental games, although this could be very elastic and even mean a street. Indeed London's Pall Mall where royal personages emerged from St James's Palace nearby to play, was named after the game. (*See also* HISTORY OF GOLF, p. 10.)

Par 'The score which a first-class player should achieve for a hole in summer conditions' (the Standard Scratch Score and handicapping scheme of the Council of National Golf Unions.) According to the same body the total of the par figures will not necessarily coincide with the Standard Scratch Score, although in many cases it will. Par for each hole is fixed as follows—250 yd (228.6 m) or less—par 3; between 251 yd and 475 yd (229.5 and 434.3 m)—par 4; 476 yd (435.2 m) and over—par 5.

Pebble Beach *See* FAMOUS AMERICAN CLUBS, p. 155.

Peg tees Golfers soon decided that long shots from the tee required some artifical aid. They placed boxes of sand on the teeing grounds, and players made a small heap on which to place the ball. This system of TEEING UP THE BALL stayed in fashion until 1928, by which time wooden peg tees with a sharp end for inserting in the ground and a small cup just large enough to hold a ball had been invented. Now many peg tees are made of plastic.

Penalty stroke A stroke added to one's score for a breach of certain of the golf rules.

Persimmon Before supplies of this wood, found in the United States, became scarce after World War II, persimmon was used to make most wooden club-heads. Now many club-heads are made of laminated woods.

Piccadilly World Match Play Tournament This famous annual tournament in which eight of the world's leading professional golfers were invited to compete, was first played in 1964. The first winner was Arnold Palmer. It was always played at the Wentworth Club, Surrey, England, but was discontinued in 1976.

Piccolo grip A method of holding the golf club in which the grip is loose, particularly the last two fingers of the left hand.

Pin *See* FLAGSTICK.

Pinehurst *See* FAMOUS AMERICAN CLUBS, p. 155.

Ping putter A putter invented in the United States which is so constructed as to make a noticeable 'click' or 'ping' when the ball is struck correctly.

Pin high The ball is said to be 'pin high' when it lands on the green in a position level with the flagstick.

Pipe That part of the shaft nearest to the head of the club, particularly in iron clubs.

Pitch A short shot played to the green and hit in such a fashion that after the ball lands it either stops or runs only a short distance.

Pitch and putt courses These exist in many parts of the world. They are often attached to driving ranges, in the grounds of hotels or at holiday resorts. The holes are usually around 100 yd (91 m) in length, each with a miniature green.

Pitch and run A short shot played to the green so that the ball rises barely off the ground and then runs towards its intended destination.

Pitch mark The mark made on the green where the ball lands. It is permissible to repair pitch marks and this should always be done so that other golfers playing behind do not have to putt over an indent in the ground.

Play-off A play-off is often the condition of an important competition when two or more players tie for first place. It can take two forms: a 'sudden death' in which the player to take the first hole outright is the winner, or a match over a certain number of stated holes.

Play short   When a golfer as a matter of strategy or safety intentionally plays short of a hazard.

Play through   If golfers are playing slowly or have been held up by certain circumstances, such as looking for a ball, then they should signal those behind them to 'play through'. In other words, they invite the following players to go in front so that they can play without hindrance.

Plugged ball   A ball is plugged when it lodges in a wet part of the course. Sometimes a local rule made by club officials allows for the ball to be lifted from the socket it has made without penalty but if no such rule exists, then the ball must be played as it lies (Rules 23, 32 and 35).

Plus   When a player has reached such a standard that his or her handicap is better than SCRATCH then they are rated as 'plus'. If a player is, say, 'plus one', then in a stroke competition one stroke has to be added to his actual score for the round. The handicapping of golfers is now so severe that there are comparatively few plus golfers. Unique in this situation were Michael Bonallack, the British amateur, and his wife, Angela. His 1972 rating was plus 2, hers plus 3.

Plus fours   Long, wide knickerbockers, for many years favoured by golfers as a style of wear on the golf course. Called 'plus fours' because, to produce the overhang, the length was normally increased by 4 in (10.2 cm). They were fully cut and gathered below the knee by elastic or buttons, and were worn with stockings. They have now gone out of fashion although some golfers still wear a modified form of plus fours.

Politician golfers   The most famous golfing politician in Britain was Mr A. J. Balfour, later Earl Balfour. He was captain of the Royal and Ancient Club in 1894, and was associated with many other clubs. His participation in the game did much to extend its popularity. Mr Harold Wilson and Mr William Whitelaw, two figures of the contemporary British political scene, are enthusiastic golfers. Mr Whitelaw is a former captain of the Royal and Ancient Club.

Portland   *See* FAMOUS AMERICAN CLUBS, p. 155.

Practice swing   It is permissible before playing a golf stroke to try a practice swing or swings.

Preferred lies   When the ball is lifted from where it is lying and placed in another position. This is done during winter in Britain when the ground is wet and golfers play what are called ·WINTER RULES·. Such rules, made by club officials, entitle a player to move his ball from a close or bad LIE to save damaging the turf on the fairway. The ball can sometimes be moved by hand, but more generally it is rolled over by using the club-head. Preferred lies are also in use in other countries as well as Britain.

Presidents, Golfing (United States)   Several United States presidents have been keen golfers, but perhaps the most enthusiastic was Dwight D. Eisenhower who presented the Eisenhower Trophy, for competition between amateur golfers of all nations. It is now known as the World Amateur Team Championship Trophy. President Ford is a golfer.

President's putter   The name of the annual competition between the Oxford and Cambridge Golfing Societies.

Press   When golfers become tense they have a tendency to try to hit the ball harder. This is known as 'to press'.

Prestwick   *See* FAMOUS BRITISH CLUBS AND COURSES, p. 147.

Pretty   A term now rarely used, to describe the fairway.

Pro-Am tournaments   These are competitions in which amateur and professional golfers partner each other.

Professional   A professional golfer is one who accepts payment for his services, say, for personal instruction, who is eligible to receive prize money in competitions, or who lends his name to advertise goods. There are now two types. Tournament professionals concentrate on playing in competitions, while club professionals concentrate on supplying the needs of the members of clubs to which they are attached. Teachers in schools whose duties include instruction in golf among other sports are not deemed to be professionals. (*See also* AMATEUR STATUS.)

Professional Golfers' Association   This body was formed in 1901 when professional golfers were just beginning to be recognized. J. H. Taylor, one of the most literate professionals of his time and others felt that professionals should be protected from clubs trying to sell equipment for their own profit and from those exploiting their professionals in other ways such as

PLATE 1 *above* St Andrews, the home of golf. The Royal and Ancient clubhouse in the background faces the first tee and the 18th green of the Old Course. *below* The Old Course, St Andrews. The famous Road Hole (surrounded by spectators) is in the foreground. The road itself, graveyard of many championship hopes, runs along the back of the green.

PLATE 2 *above* An unusual picture of five times Open Champion Peter Thomson of Australia on the 18th tee on the Old Course at St Andrews. *below* American Johnny Miller driving from the first tee at Troon in the 1973 Open Championship, watched by Tom Weiskopf, the eventual winner.

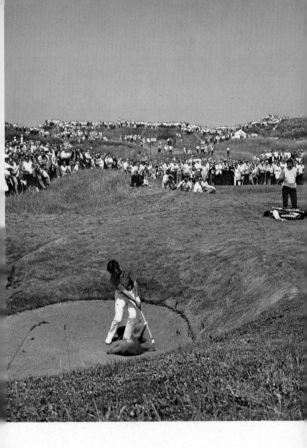

PLATE 3   Tony Jacklin playing from a bunker in a practice round for the Open Championship at Muirfield in 1972. He finished in third place behind Trevino and Nicklaus.

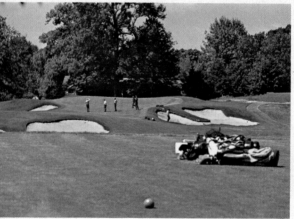

PLATE 4 *above* The clubhouse and the 18th fairway of the famous Old Troon Championship course, venue of several Open Championships.
below The par three 10th hole on one of the most famous and spectacular courses in the U.S.A., the West course at Winged Foot.

PLATE 5 *above*
One of the most
colourful of all
professional golfers,
Lee Trevino, winner
of both the United
States and British
Open
Championships, as
well as many other
major events.

left Neil Coles, over
the years, has been
Britain's most
consistent golfer. Of
major British events
only the Open
Championship has
eluded him.

PLATE 6   Few British courses have a more attractive setting
for their first tee than Fulford, York, scene of Benson & Hedges
Festival of Golf.

PLATE 7 *above* The American J. C. Snead, nephew of the legendary Sam Snead and himself a professional of distinction. Has played for the United States in Ryder Cup matches. *below* On the left Tom Weiskopf with Britain's Peter Oosterhuis who does not seem too satisfied with the result of his shot.

above A scene during the Madrid Open at the R.A.C., Madrid. Golf in Spain is becoming increasingly popular.

PLATE 8

left A view of the Henry Cotton designed course at Val do Lobo in the Algarve province of Portugal. The course has many magnificent holes.

having their services without payment. Taylor was the first chairman and James Braid was the first captain. Since its formation in London the association soon spread throughout Britain and now most professionals are members. The P.G.A. looks after the interests of its members and is responsible for the Ryder Cup match played against the United States professionals every two years. The P.G.A. Tournament Players' Division controls golf tournaments.

Professional Golfers' Association of America This body was formed in 1916, much later than its British counterpart. It serves the same purpose as the British association. The United States P.G.A. has its headquarters and own course at Palm Beach Gardens, Florida, where each year every professional wishing to play on the tournament circuit has to undergo a course and a golf test before he can obtain what is called his 'ticket'. The United States P.G.A. has its own championship and organizes Ryder Cup matches when they are played in the United States.

Professional Golfers' Co-operative Association This organization was formed in 1920 to act as a link between golf equipment manufacturers and professional golfers. Its headquarters are at Putney, London, and it has several branches throughout the country. Its customers not only include professionals in Britain, but also many professionals overseas.

Public (municipal) golf courses Throughout Britain and also in the United States as well as in some other countries there are public courses. Such courses are owned and controlled by local authorities and anyone is free to play on them on payment of what is known as a green fee, i.e. payment for a round or for a day's golf. Scotland is particularly lucky in its public courses such as those at St Andrews, Carnoustie, Monifieth, Leven, Troon and elsewhere. Many public courses have clubs whose members enjoy the benefits and privileges of their own private club-house.

Pull When a shot is pulled, the ball can set off on the correct line and then gradually veer towards the left. The difference between 'draw' and 'pull' is that a 'draw' is intentional and a 'pull' is not.

Push   To hit the ball to the right. The opposite of PULL.

Putt   The stroke used on or near the putting surface or green. A putter has a straight face and a shaft shorter than other clubs (except in a few instances). The most popular type is either a centre-shafted putter in which the shaft meets the club-head at the top of the centre of the head, or a blade putter in which the shaft is joined to the end of the head.

Putting green   The grass areas on a golf course which has been specially cut round the hole. The term is not so often used now, 'green' being most common. The term is now mainly applied to the practice putting greens which can be found at most clubs.

Quit   A term used more in the United States than in Britain. 'To quit on a shot' is not to carry out the stroke with determination. This frequently happens when a golfer is undecided as to which club he should play or which line of action he should take.

Rabbit   The expression used to describe a golfer with a long handicap or who has no handicap because of the poor standard of his play. The opposite of TIGER.

Record score   The lowest and hence the best score on a course can only be regarded as such if it is achieved in a competition where a card is duly authenticated.

Referee   The person put in charge of a golf match, and whose duties consist solely of deciding questions on the rules of the game.

Rejected clubs   From time to time the Royal and Ancient Club has golf clubs submitted to it for approval. Many of these are rejected, and at the headquarters at St Andrews there is a large number of them—some look very strange.

Reverse overlapping grip   Used by some golfers when putting. Instead of the little finger of the right hand overlapping the index finger of the left hand, the index finger of the left hand overlaps the little finger of the right hand. The aim is to achieve a firmer grip of the club with the left hand.

Rim (1) The edge of the hole. (2) The expression 'to rim the hole' means that the ball runs round the lip of the hole and fails to drop.

Road Hole The famous 17th hole on the Old Course at St Andrews. The hole is so named because a road runs alongside the back of the green. The hole is still a hazardous one but not so much as it was when the road, now smooth, was a track. The road is not out of bounds and any ball landing on it must be played (Pl. 1).

Rough The Rules of Golf do not recognize the existence of rough. In 1890 in the Badminton Library book on Golf, a golf course was said to be 'that portion of the links, on which the game ought to be played, generally bounded on either side by rough ground or other hazards.' In the passage of time the words 'rough ground' have been curtailed to 'rough'.

Round of golf A round of golf, unless otherwise authorized by an official committee, should be composed of 18 holes.

Round, To play a To play all the holes of the course.

Round Robin A type of competition, more popular in the United States than in Britain in which players meet each other as in a league.

Royal and Ancient Golf Club of St Andrews The ruling body of the game so far as most countries of the world are concerned except United States. Golf was being played on the links at St Andrews by 1552 but it was not until 14th May 1754 that 'twenty-two Noblemen and Gentlemen, being admirers of the ancient and healthful exercise of golf' met together to form a golfing society, and to draw up rules under which they were to play. At the same meeting the 'twenty-two' also decided to subscribe five shillings each towards the purchase of a silver club to be put up for competition to all golfers. One provision was that the winner had to affix to the club a silver ball. To recompense him for the outlay, the entrance money was to be his.

The Society of St Andrews Golfers, as it was generally known, continued to flourish and hold frequent meetings, but it had no home and the players, after their golfing competitions, adjourned to the Black Bull Tavern owned by a golfing enthusiast, Bailie Glass. The hostelry of Mrs Adamson was also frequented. The Society dinners were held at the Black Bull and the sum charged was one shilling!

In 1835 there was formed at St Andrews the Union Club, consisting of members of the Archers' Club and any golfers who cared to join. The club rented premises for the annual sum of £5. Around the same time the Society of St Andrews Golfers became 'Royal' and took the name 'Royal and Ancient', King William IV being persuaded to give it his patronage, having already given it to the Perth Golfing Society.

The next event of great importance in the history of the club came in 1853 when the Union Club, with whom the Royal and Ancient had close ties although they were in no way merged, decided to have a club-house of its own. Many individuals were members of both clubs and most of them ardently wished for an amalgamation, and it finally came about in 1853. By this time the Union Club had begun building their club-house which stands in St Andrews today. Although it has seen vast alterations, these have not destroyed the appearance of what was then, and still is, a handsome building.

The Honourable Company of Edinburgh Golfers had drawn up the first set of rules and now the St Andrews golfers drew up theirs. Gradually the St Andrews rules found favour with golfers until they became those under which golf all over the world was played.

When the Open Championship Belt was won outright by 'Young Tommy' Morris and the competition ceased, the Royal and Ancient Club joined with Prestwick and the Honourable Company in presenting a new trophy to be played for in turn on the courses of the three clubs.

The Royal and Ancient, on an approach from Hoylake in 1886, took over the running of the Amateur Championship, and now organizes that event in addition to the Open Championship and various other championships and matches.

Although its rules were being used in Britain and many other countries, it was not until 1924 that the Home Unions agreed to make the Royal and Ancient Club the ruling body of the game in Britain. On consultation with Commonwealth countries, they also agreed to bide by these rules. Now any queries regarding rules can be referred to St Andrews.

The Royal and Ancient Club works closely with the United States Golf Association on all matters relating to rules and other aspects of the game.

The Royal and Ancient Club captain is elected every year. Policy is decided by a number of committees. There is a highly skilled staff controlled by an executive known as the secretary. (*See also* HISTORY OF GOLF, p. 11 and BRITISH AMATEUR CHAMPIONSHIP.)

Royal Birkdale *See* FAMOUS BRITISH CLUBS AND COURSES, p. 148.

Royal Blackheath *See* FAMOUS BRITISH CLUBS AND COURSES, p. 148.

Royal Burgess Society of Edinburgh Golfers *See* FAMOUS BRITISH CLUBS AND COURSES, p. 148.

Royal Cinque Ports *See* FAMOUS BRITISH CLUBS AND COURSES, p. 148.

Royal golf clubs
England and Channel Islands
    Royal Ashdown Forest, Forest Row, Sussex
    Royal Birkdale, Southport, Lancashire
    Royal Blackheath, Eltham, London S.E.9
    Royal Cinque Ports, Deal, Kent
    Royal Cromer, Cromer, Norfolk
    Royal Eastbourne, Eastbourne, Sussex
    Royal Epping Forest, Chingford, Essex
    Royal Guernsey, L'Ancresse, Guernsey
    Royal Jersey, Grouville, Jersey
    Royal Liverpool, Hoylake, Cheshire
    Royal Lytham and St Annes, St Annes-on-Sea, Lancashire
    Royal Mid-Surrey, Richmond, Surrey
    Royal North Devon, Westward Ho!, Devon
    Royal Norwich, Norwich, Norfolk
    Royal St George's, Sandwich, Kent
    Royal West Norfolk, Brancaster, Norfolk
    Royal Wimbledon, Wimbledon Common, London S.W.19
    Royal Winchester, Winchester, Hampshire
    Royal Worlington, Worlington, Suffolk
Ireland
    Royal Belfast, Craigavad, Co. Down
    Royal County Down, Newcastle, Co. Down
    Royal Dublin, Dollymount, Dublin
    Royal Portrush, Co. Antrim

Scotland

Royal Aberdeen, Balgownie, Aberdeenshire
Royal Albert, Montrose, Angus
Royal and Ancient, St Andrews, Fife
Royal Burgess Golfing Society, Barnton, Edinburgh
Royal Craggan, Braemar, Aberdeenshire
Royal Dornoch, Dornoch, Sutherland
Duff House Royal, Banff, Banffshire
Royal Musselburgh, Prestonpans, Midlothian
Royal Perth Golfing Society, Perth, Perthshire
Royal Tarlair, Macduff, Banffshire

Wales

Royal Porthcawl, Porthcawl, Glamorgan
Royal St Davids, Harlech, Merioneth

Africa

Royal Cape, Wynberg, Cape Province
Royal Durban, Durban, Natal
Royal Johannesburg, Johannesburg, Transvaal
Royal Port Alfred, Kowie West, Cape Province
Royal Nairobi, Kenya
Royal Salisbury, Rhodesia

Australia

Royal Adelaide, Seaton, South Australia
Royal Canberra, Canberra, Capital Territory
Royal Fremantle, Fremantle, West Australia
Royal Hobart, Hobart, Tasmania
Royal Melbourne, Black Rock, Victoria
Royal Perth, Perth, West Australia
Royal Queensland, Brisbane, Queensland
Royal Sydney, Sydney, New South Wales

Canada

Royal Colwood, Victoria, British Columbia
Royal Montreal, Montreal, Quebec
Royal Ottawa, Ottawa, Quebec
Royal Quebec, Boischatel, Quebec

India

Royal Bombay, Bombay Gymkhana, Bombay
Royal Calcutta, Tollygunge, Calcutta
Royal Western India, Nasik

Other British-created 'Royal' clubs are: Royal Colombo, Sri Lanka (Ceylon), Royal Hong Kong, Royal Malta.

There are several 'Royal' clubs throughout the world created by royal houses other than British.

Royal Golfers   The first royal golfer was King James IV of Scotland who was a keen exponent of the game. In 1503 there is a record of accounts to the royal household for the purchase of golf balls. His son James V also played golf and his daughter, Mary, Queen of Scots, took up the game. It was her son James VI of Scotland and I of England who brought golf to England when he became King of England and Scotland. He established his court at Greenwich and played golf there and at Blackheath. James's two sons, Prince Henry, who died at an early age, and his brother, Charles I, were both golfers. Charles I was playing golf on the Links of Leith when news was brought to him of the Irish Rebellion. Charles's son, James II, was a keen player who took part in a famous match partnering the shoemaker, John Patersone, against two English noblemen for a substantial stake. Patersone was well rewarded for his contribution to the successful outcome and as a result was able to build his own house in Edinburgh.

Strangely enough William IV, the monarch who gave the Royal patronage to the Perth Society and the St Andrews golfers, never played the game but took a great interest in it. He presented the King William Medal to the Royal and Ancient Club.

King Edward VII became captain of the Royal and Ancient, as did his brother, Prince Leopold. However, King Edward VII played mostly abroad, at Cannes, apart perhaps from the private course at Windsor. He did not 'play himself in' as Captain of the Royal and Ancient as other captains have done.

Perhaps the best known and most talented of Britain's royal golfers were the two brothers, King George VI and the Duke of Windsor. Both played a great deal, mostly at Sunningdale and both became proficient. They were captains of the Royal and Ancient Club. During World War II the professional, Dai Rees, played with King George VI.

Overseas the best royal golfers have been King Leopold of Belgium and his son, King Baudouin. Both have appeared in competitions and King Baudouin played in a Pro-Am tournament at Gleneagles in Scotland. A Russian, the Grand Duke Michael, who spent most of his life outside his own country, was a keen golfer and founded the Cannes Golf Club in the South of France, around 1890. King Hassan of Morocco is a keen golfer.

Royal golf clubs: Oldest   The first royal golf club was the Royal Perth Golfing Society which was accorded royal patronage by William IV in 1833. The club was founded nine years before that date. The Royal and Ancient Golf Club of St Andrews became 'Royal' a little later.

Rubber core ball   *See* HASKELL BALL.

Rub of the green   Any interference by an outside agency with the ball while it is in motion. Rub of the green might also be interpreted as a stroke of fate or act of God. The expression is used in a philosophical manner.

Rules of Golf   The Rules of Golf drawn up by the Royal and Ancient Club are the rules by which golfers of most countries of the world abide.

Rules of amateur status   *See* AMATEUR STATUS.

Rules of Golf Committee   In 1896, after representations from competitors in the Amateur Championship, the Royal and Ancient Golf Club established a committee to deal with all aspects of the rules of golf. The committee still exists and is composed of twelve members of the Royal and Ancient and eight other members representing golf bodies in the British Isles and overseas. The committee has a close contact with the United States Golf Association which has its own code of rules. Fundamentally, golf competitions all over the world are played according to the rules laid down by the Royal and Ancient Rules of Golf Committee. (*See also* ROYAL AND ANCIENT GOLF CLUB OF ST ANDREWS.)

Run   The distance the ball travels after hitting the ground.

Run-up   A short low shot to the green.

Rut iron   A club designed specifically for removing the ball from ruts, wheel marks, etc. The club is no longer in use.

Ryder Cup   A match between members of the British Professional Golfers' Association and members of the American Professional Golfers' Association. It is played every two years, alternately in Britain and United States at different venues for each match, for a trophy presented by a golf enthusiast, the late Samuel Ryder, and was inaugurated in 1927 at Worcester, Mass., after an unofficial game between British and American professionals at Wentworth in 1926, won by Great Britain by 13 matches to 1. (For results *see* p. 192.)

St Andrews   *See* FAMOUS BRITISH CLUBS AND COURSES, p. 151.

St Andrews Golf Club (U.S.A.)   *See* FAMOUS AMERICAN CLUBS, p. 156.

St Andrews Trophy   This trophy is for the two-yearly match between the amateurs of the British Isles and the Continent of Europe. It is played alternately in the British Isles and on the Continent.

St George's Challenge Cup   Probably the oldest open amateur stroke play competition. It began in 1888, and is played at the St George's Club, Sandwich, over 36 holes.

Sammy   The name of a golf club long since extinct. It resembled a JIGGER and was used mainly for little shots to the green.

Sand iron   A club used to play out of bunkers. It has a deep face with a flange. The name has fallen into disuse, its modern name being the BLASTER or sand wedge.

Schenectady putter   The first of the centre-shafted putters, i.e. putters in which the shaft is joined to the club-head at the centre of the top of the head. The inventor is believed to have been an American named Wright. In 1904 Walter Travis, an extrovert Australian, used this putter in winning the British Amateur Championship at Sandwich and thereafter it was banned in Britain until 1952 when this type of putter was made legal.

Sclaff   To scrape the ground before the club-head makes contact with the ball. The result is that the ball scurries along the ground.

Score   The total number of strokes recorded by a golfer during a round.

Score cards   The first score cards were used in the Open Championship in 1865 and they are now used in all stroke play competitions. At the start of the round cards are exchanged, A giving his score card to B, B giving his to A. Each player has to mark the other's card but the player whose name is on the card is responsible for making sure that it is correctly marked by his partner or marker. The card has to be signed by the player whose score is registered on it and then countersigned by the marker. Penalty for handing in a wrongly marked card is disqualification.

Scotch foursomes   The name for FOURSOMES in the United States.

Scottish Amateur Championship   The Scottish Amateur Championship is a comparatively new competition considering the length of time the game has been played in Scotland. It was begun in 1922. It is open to Scottish amateur golfers (either by birth or if one parent is Scottish). No golfer who has played in the English, Irish or Welsh championships is eligible. It is an annual match play championship and the venues vary each year.

Scottish Golf Union   The union, as with the other home unions, administers the game in its own country. It organizes the Scottish Amateur Championship, and the Scottish Stroke Play Championship. It is responsible for the selection of Scottish international teams and generally fosters the game throughout the country. It was the first home union to have its championship commercially sponsored (in 1973).

Scratch   A golfer who can play to the scratch or near par score of the course. The scratch score is fixed according to the length of the course measured from medal tees in summer conditions. The Standard Scratch Score and Handicapping Scheme of the Council of National Golf Unions is the yardstick from which all handicaps come. The minimum requirement of a golfer to obtain or keep his handicap of scratch is that he should have played to that handicap, which in effect is zero, in at least five competitions during the calendar year by returning a gross score equal to or less than the scratch score of each course on the day concerned.

Semi-rough   That part of the course where the grass is not so long as in the ROUGH. Semi-rough is usually between the edge of the fairway and the rough proper.

Senior Golfers' Society of Great Britain   An exclusive society formed in 1926. Only golfers over 55 are eligible for membership. It holds frequent golf meetings, plays senior golfers from other countries and on occasions sends teams overseas. There are senior golfers' societies in several overseas countries including the United States.

Set   A set of clubs is limited to 14. Until just before World War II golfers could carry any number of clubs, and a player once carried 19. There is no particular reason why 14 should have been selected.

Shanking   When the ball is hit off the heel of the club, that part where the club-head joins the shaft, and the ball flies off at a tangent.

Short set   To encourage new golfers, some manufacturers market a set usually of seven clubs which is called a 'short set'.

Shutting the face   *See* HOODING THE CLUB.

Skying the ball   When the ball goes straight in the air usually with a wooden club, there are two main reasons—the wrong transference of weight and a loose arm action.

Slice (cut)   To strike the ball in such a manner that it curves to the right. The main cause of a slice is in bringing the club-face across the back of the ball from outside to inside, thus cutting across the ball. *See* DRAW: FADE, CONTROLLED.

Slow play   All golfers must keep their place on a golf course, and if delayed must allow players following to proceed. To fail to do so is to indulge in slow play. *See also* ETIQUETTE.

Socketing   *See* SHANKING.

Southerly course, Most   The most southerly golf course in the world is one of nine holes in the Falkland Islands.

Spade mashie   The old name for a deep-faced mashie, somewhere between a mashie and a niblick. In fact some old golfers referred to this club as a MASHIE NIBLICK.

Speed of golf ball   The last known tests to register the speed of a golf ball revealed that the speed of the club-head at the moment of impact was 110.5 miles (177.8 km) per hour. That would give the ball an estimated speed of approximately 125 miles (201 km) per hour. The tests were carried out some years ago, and with modern equipment the speed of both club-head and ball would be faster.

Split-handed putting   When the two hands gripping the

putter are entirely separate and in most cases some distance apart. No department of the game has more experiments devoted to it than putting, and split-handed putting is a method favoured by some.

Spoon A wooden club with a deeper face and a shorter shaft than its bigger brother, the BRASSIE. Now almost obsolete, its place has been taken by a No 3 wood. It was invented to send the ball away from the close fairways to be found on Scottish seaside courses. (*See also* BAFFY.)

Square (1) Refers to the club-head or stance when it is square to the line of the intended flight of the ball. (2) *See* ALL SQUARE.

Stableford System A system of scoring invented by Dr Frank Stableford, of the Wallasey Club, who died in 1959. Dr Stableford felt that many competitions were dull and he evolved his own type of scoring in 1932. A Stableford competition is played against BOGEY, and competitors, instead of being up or down to bogey, are awarded points thus:

For hole done in one over the official score of the hole	1 point
For hole done in official score	2 points
For hole done in one under official score	3 points
For hole done in two under official score	4 points
For hole done in three under official score	5 points

No points are given for holes done in more than one over the fixed score. The same applies to a hole which the competitor did not complete.

If the Stableford competition is a single, i.e. each player playing for himself, then the handicap allowed is seven-eighths of the full handicap, e.g. if the full handicap was eight then the allowance would be seven. The handicap is taken at the appropriate holes but this can vary, for some clubs allow the handicap allowance to be made at the end of the round. If the competition is a foursome the partners receive seven-sixteenths of their combined handicaps. If, when dividing the joint handicaps, a half-stroke occurs then the partners gain some advantage, because one cannot have a half-stroke handicap. That means the handicap, which might have been five-and-a-half, goes up to six.

Stance   The positioning of the feet before playing a golf stroke. Three stances might be described as orthodox—the open, the square, and the closed. The first is when the left foot is drawn back from the intended flight of the ball; the second is when both feet are square to the intended line and the third when the left foot is forward of the intended direction of the ball. Other stances, such as an uphill stance or a downhill stance, are governed by the undulations of the ground.

Standard Scratch Score   The score in which a SCRATCH golfer is expected to go round a golf course playing from the medal (or competition) tees in summer conditions. The Standard Scratch Score is fixed according to the length of the course. The body responsible for laying down conditions for a standard scratch score is the Council of National Golf Unions. The S.S.S., as it is known, is calculated on the length of a course. Owing to differences in terrain and other conditions, the S.S.S. is not always as accurate an assessment of a golf course as it might be, but with so many courses of varying terrain, to achieve one hundred per cent accuracy would be impossible. But generally the S.S.S. has proved the best solution to the problems.

Steal   An opponent is said to 'steal' a hole when he wins it unexpectedly.

Steamy   An expression used to describe a shot which has sent the ball careering past the hole.

Steel shafts   Steel shafts were made legal in Britain in 1929, after they had been in use for some time in the United States. Various clubs with shafts of iron or steel had been invented in Britain long before 1929, but had not found favour. Hickory shafts held sway for many years, although attempts had been made to popularize shafts made of various other materials such as cane. The first man to invent steel shafts may have been Thomas Horsburgh of the Baberton Club near Edinburgh who patented such clubs as early as the mid-nineties. But Horsburgh could do little with his clubs as they were banned.

Stroke   (1) The action made by a golfer when hitting the ball. (2) A player of a higher handicap receives from a player of a lower handicap a stroke at certain holes or on the round.

Stroke hole   A hole at which one player receives a stroke, in accordance with the handicap rules. On every score card issued by golf clubs there is a stroke index stating at which particular holes strokes can be taken.

Stroke (medal) play   A competition, also known as medal play, in which the results are determined by the number of strokes played. The winner of such a competition is the player who goes round in the least number of strokes, be it SCRATCH or handicap, according to the competition.

Stroke Play: First competition   The first recorded stroke play competition was organized by the Company of Edinburgh Golfers in 1744. The competition was for a silver club presented by the City of Edinburgh.

Stymie   When the ball of one player rests in a direct line between the hole and the ball of an opponent in match play, the balls being less than 6 in (15.2 cm) apart. The stymie, which could be either intentional or unintentional, was abolished in Britain and in the United States in 1951. The decision to abolish the stymie was brought about by strong press criticism when in the final of the English Amateur Championship at Hunstanton in 1951 G. P. Roberts laid his opponent a stymie on the 39th green and by so doing, either by accident or design, won the championship.

Sucker   Describes a ball lodged in wet ground.

Sunningdale System   A system of scoring which has never become universally popular. It involves giving an opponent who becomes two holes down, a stroke at the next hole. If the opponent halves the hole, he receives another stroke; if the receiver of the stroke wins, the pair play the next hole level; if the giver of the stroke wins, he gives another stroke at the next hole, and so on. The object is to make the game as close as possible.

Sweetspot   The sweetspot on a club-head is that part with which the ball must be struck to achieve the best results. It is usually the centre but can vary according to design.

Swilcan   The famous burn or stream which runs across the first and the 18th fairways on the Old Course at St Andrews.

Swing   The motion of the club made by a golfer before and after hitting the ball.

Swing weight   Today golf clubs are made in a sophisticated manner and manufacturers, in order to gauge the correct balance of a golf club shaft, put it through tests of which swing weight is one. It not only ensures that the shafts are correct in relation to the weight of the heads, but that the shafts are related to those of clubs in the same set.

Take-away   The first movement of the swing when the club-head is taken away from the ball. If the 'take-away' is incorrect, then the chances are that the stroke will not be satisfactory.

Taylor, J. H.   *See* TRIUMVIRATE, THE GREAT.

Tee   (1) Originally the area reserved for striking the ball at the start of a hole was known as the teeing ground and was a rectangular area of two club lengths in depth. That still holds good today. The word is generally thought to have come from the Gaelic word meaning 'house'. A common expression at golf clubs is 'See you on the first tee', not 'See you on the first teeing ground'. (2) Tee can also mean the peg on which the ball is placed before driving off. (*See also* PEG TEES.)

Teeing up the ball   The act of placing the ball on the PEG TEE or tee peg.

Tee peg   *See* PEG TEES.

Television of golf events   Television of golf events is now commonplace all over the world. Such tournaments as the British Open Championship and the U.S. Open Championship are shown live in various countries. The first time the U.S. Open Championship was televised was in 1954 when the event was played at the Olympic Club, San Francisco. The British Open Championship was televised for the first time from St Andrews in 1957.

Tempo   The tempo of the golf swing must be achieved with a smooth rhythm if a correct stroke is to be played. If too fast then the chances are a bad stroke will result. The degree to which tempo can be slowed depends on the individual.

Texas wedge   An American term used for a putter when it is employed to play a shot from off the green. When it became popular to play high dropping shots to the green, golfers in Texas where the ground is often dry found they could obtain more accurate results by hitting the ball along the ground with a putter. In time the term 'Texas wedge' came into being.

Threesome   Three-ball matches. (*See also* MATCHES, KINDS OF.)

Tie   (1) A match between two or four players which has ended level after all the holes have been completed. (2) The word is also sometimes used instead of 'match' e.g. 'A first tie was between . . .'

Tiger   A player with a high degree of skill and a low handicap. The opposite of RABBIT

Tiger country   *See* JUNGLE COUNTRY.

Timing   If a good stroke is to be played the ball must be hit when the club-head is moving at its fastest possible speed. If it is, then the timing is correct and no effort has been wasted by the incorrect movement of the club-head.

Top   To 'top' the ball is to hit on or near the top. The result is that the ball runs along the ground.

Topspin   When the ball is hit correctly with one of the longer woods, such as a No 1 or No 2 wood, the ball flies with a downward revolving motion during its flight. The result is that on landing the ball rolls forward. Topspin can also be imparted to the ball when it is *topped*.

Track iron   An obsolete expression to describe a club once used for playing from a rough track or rut.

Tradesman's entrance   *See* BACK DOOR.

Trajectory, of the ball   The flight of the ball through the air. For example, the ball may have a high or a low trajectory.

Trap   An American word describing the hazard known to British golfers as a BUNKER.

Triumvirate, The great   At the turn of the century three British professionals did more to popularize golf than any other players. They were James Braid, a Scotsman from Earlsferry, John Henry Taylor, born in Northam, Devon, and Harry Vardon, a Channel Islander from Jersey. Between them they all but monopolized the British Open Championship from 1894 to 1914. Together they won sixteen Open championships, Vardon winning six and the other two five each.

Trolley   *See* CADDIE CAR.

Twitch   When a golfer suffers from an attack of nerves to such a degree that on the putting green he cannot strike the ball correctly; he usually does so with a quick, jerky motion.

United States Amateur Championship   The United States Amateur Championship is an annual event which has been played since 1895. (There had been two unofficial championships before that date.) The first winner of the championship was Charles Blair Macdonald at Newport, Rhode Island. He was born in New York but was sent to St Andrews University to complete his education and became interested in golf. He was the father-in-law of H. J. Whigham who followed him as champion for the next two years. As well as being a good golfer he was keenly interested in the legislation of the game, was a founder member of the United States Golf Association, and had much to do with the rules of golf decisions in the early days of American golf. The first non-American to win the U.S. Amateur Championship was the eccentric Australian, Walter Travis in 1900. The only British winner to date was the late Harold Hilton in 1911. In 1936 the Scottish amateur, the late Jack McLean, came near to winning the title when at Garden City he was beaten by Johnny Fischer at the 37th hole. If it had not been for a STYMIE at the 34th hole McLean might well have won.

The championship was played by MATCH PLAY up to 1964. From 1965 to 1972 it was a stroke play event, then reverted to match play. (For winners *see* p. 182. *See also* HISTORY OF AMERICAN GOLF, p. 21.)

United States Golf, History of   *See* HISTORY OF AMERICAN GOLF, p. 19.

United States Masters Tournament   *See*   MASTERS TOURNAMENT.

United States Open Championship   After one or two false starts the first United States Open Championship was played at Newport, Rhode Island, in 1895 and was won by a young Englishman, Horace Rawlins. Some people maintain, however, that the event began a year before, and that the first United States champion was really Willie Dunn. Dunn's victory was by

MATCH PLAY. Since that first tentative venture all the championships have been by STROKE PLAY. The first American to win the championship was John McDermott in 1911. McDermott also won in 1912 and the next championship was one of the most famous of them all. Harry Vardon, who had previously won the title in 1902, was making another bid and found himself in a three-way tie with his fellow countryman, Ted Ray, and a young 20-year-old American amateur, Francis Ouimet. To the great surprise of all Ouimet, who later became a distinguished legislator and a Captain of the Royal and Ancient Club, won the title. He was the first amateur to do so. However, the most famous amateur to take the title was Robert Tyre Jones, Jr, who won on four occasions. The last amateur to win the championship was Johnnie Goodman in 1933. (For winners *see* p. 179.)

United States Professional Golfers' Association Championship This championship was started in 1916, the year of the formation of the United States Professional Golfers' Association. Originally it was a MATCH PLAY event but in 1958 it became STROKE (MEDAL) PLAY over four rounds. Only one overseas golfer, Gary Player from South Africa, has won the event. (For winners *see* p. 189.)

United States Women's Amateur Championship Inaugurated in 1895 by the United States Golf Association and first played at Meadowbrook, New York. The first winner was Mrs Charles Brown who won with an 18-hole total of 132 from twelve other competitors. That was the first and only time the event has been held under STROKE PLAY conditions. There have been three British champions, Miss Dorothy Campbell, Miss Gladys Ravenscroft and Miss Pam Barton. Miss Marlene Stewart of Canada and Mlle Catherine Lacoste of France were other non-American winners. (For winners *see* p. 185.)

United States Women's Open Championship In the United States there are a large number of women professionals who have their own circuit of tournaments. In 1946 their own Open Championship was inaugurated, the winner being the former amateur, Patty Berg.

Former British and U.S. Open Champion Tony Jacklin playing in the Swiss Open at Crans-sur-Sierre. Jacklin held the U.S. and the British Open Championship at the same time, having won the British title in 1969 and the U.S. Open Championship in 1970 (the two periods overlapping)

(*left*) Johnny Miller,
one of the great
American golf stars
of the 70s. He may
become the all-time
record money
winner. (*right*)
Maurice Bembridge
is one of the most
consistent of British
professionals, and
the one who travels
farthest in his
search for success.
He has a good
record at home and
overseas

(left) Jack Nicklaus, winner of all the major championships of Britain and the United States. In 1973 he established a new record for earnings by winning $316,000 in competitions. (right) Peter Oosterhuis, who after being successful in Europe, decided to campaign in the United States. He was leading British professional in 1971–4, and was awarded the Vardon Trophy for this feat

University match   Many golf matches are played between British universities, but the best known is that between Oxford and Cambridge. The match was first played in 1878.

Upright swing   A swing in which the arc made by the club-head on its upward journey is less wide than the arc formed by golfers who take the club-head back from the ball along the ground until they can do so no longer and retain proper balance. Some golfers are for an upright swing and some against. Those against say that a full arc of the club-head is essential. Those for maintain that the speed of the club-head is generated on the downswing, and that they can achieve this more easily with an upright swing. Much depends on the height of the golfer. A tall, powerful golfer would derive better results from an upright swing than would a small, slightly built golfer.

Valley of Sin   Just in front of the 18th hole on the Old Course at St Andrews is a deep hollow. Often a player going for the green finds that he has not hit the ball hard enough and that it rolls back into the hollow with disastrous results—hence the name, Valley of Sin.

Vardon, Harry   *See* TRIUMVIRATE, THE GREAT.

Vardon grip   *See* GRIPS, TYPES OF.

Vardon Trophy   Harry Vardon, one of the greatest golfers in the history of the game, has his name perpetuated in the Harry Vardon Trophy, awarded to the member of the British Professional Golfers' Association who has the best average score after competing in all the major tournaments of the year. The British Vardon Trophy dates from 1937, the year of his death. There is also an American Vardon Trophy.

V   A technical term to describe the angle between the thumb and forefinger when gripping a club. Most professionals when teaching a pupil demonstrate that the 'V's made by the thumb and forefinger of each hand should point towards the right shoulder.

Waggle   Moving the club-head backwards and forwards over the ball preparatory to hitting it. There are two reasons for doing this, firstly to help the player relax and secondly to generate club-head speed. Some golfers dispense with the waggle but they are few. The greatest wagglers of all time were the champions Sandy Herd and Fred Daly. Daly had numerous waggles with every club in his bag, including the putter.

Walker, Arthur   The only non-native Englishman to win the English Amateur Championship, which he did in 1957. He qualified to play, for although born in South Africa, his mother was English.

Walker Cup   This famous trophy is played for every two years between the amateurs of the British Isles and those of the United States. The donor was Mr George H. Walker, a former president of the United States Golf Association, and the first Walker Cup Match was played at Long Island in 1922, but the first international match involving teams from the British Isles and the United States was played in 1921 on the links of the Royal Liverpool Club at Hoylake, where the United States won. Played alternately in Britain and United States. (For results *see* p. 190.)

Walker Cup and Ryder Cup: Played in both   Three players have played for the British Isles in both the Walker Cup and the Ryder Cup, Norman Drew, Peter Townsend and Peter Oosterhuis. Five Americans have played in both, Tommy Aaron, Fred Hass, Gene Littler, Jack Nicklaus and Ken Venturi. The Scottish-born Tommy Armour, a famous amateur before he turned professional, played in the first amateur international against the United States and then later played for the United States in the Ryder Cup match.

Water hazards   *See* HAZARDS.

Wedge   The most modern club in the golfer's bag, it has superseded the niblick. It dates back to 1932 when American professional, Gene Sarazen made for himself a deep-faced club with a flanged sole for the purpose of hitting out of sand traps. That club became the forerunner of the wedge which today is very lofted and heavier than the niblick or No 9 iron. Its weight, its lofted face and flanged sole enables an expert golfer to put the ball in the air so that it drops close to the hole and on landing stops. The range of a wedge is around 100 yd (91 m). (*See also* SAND IRON: BLASTER.)

Welsh Amateur Championship   The second oldest of the

home championships. It was instituted in 1895. It is match play and is held annually. Competitors must have at least one parent of Welsh parentage and must not have played in the English, Irish or Scottish Amateur Championships in the past fifteen years.

Welsh Golfing Union   Formed in 1895, it has as its aims the furthering of golf in Wales and also Monmouthshire. It organizes the Welsh Amateur Championship and keeps in close contact with the other national bodies and with the Royal and Ancient Club.

Whipping   The wax thread, and even earlier the thick un-waxed thread used for binding the joint of the shaft and the head. The same material also bound the foot of the grip to the shaft. Now the binding is effected by more modern methods using plastic materials.

Whippy   The degree of tension or movement in a golf shaft.

Winter rules   The rules which golf club committees put into operation to protect their courses in bad weather.

Woods   The clubs in a golf set which have heads made of wood or, occasionally, a synthetic substance.

Woof   *See* BOWF.

World Amateur Team Championship Trophy   Formerly known as the Eisenhower Trophy. This trophy was presented by former U.S. President, Dwight D. Eisenhower, and was first played for at St Andrews in 1958. Teams from any country may compete, each consisting of four players. The competition is held in a different country every four years. The best three four-round scores count in the final reckoning.

World Cup (formerly Canada Cup)   For professional teams from any country. Each team consists of two players and the winners are those who have the best four-round aggregate. There is also an individual prize. The trophy was presented by an American industrialist, the late John J. Hopkins, to foster good relations between the golf professionals of all countries. It was first played for in Montreal, and is now played annually on different courses in various countries of the world.

World Series   An important event played at Akron, Ohio.

Only invited players may compete, these being the British Open Champion, the U.S. Open Champion, the U.S. Masters Champion and the U.S. P.G.A. Champion.

Worplesdon Mixed Foursomes The most famous mixed foursomes tournament in the world, played every autumn at the Worplesdon Club, Surrey. It was begun in 1921 and for many years was dominated by Miss Joyce Wethered, later Lady Heathcoat Amory, who won with a variety of partners.

Youngest British Amateur champion John Beharrell, who won at Troon in 1956, and Bobby Cole (South Africa), who won at Carnoustie ten years later, were both 18 when they took the titles. On the day each of them won they were exactly the same age.

Youngest British Boys' champion F. Morris who won the title in 1961 and P. M. Townsend, who won the following year, were both 15.

Youngest British Girls' champion Miss Nancy Jupp of Longniddry won the British Girls' Championship at Stoke Poges when she was 13. The first handicap she had in golf was four. After giving up golf for some years she returned to the game and became a Middlesex county player and Norwegian Ladies' champion. She is now organizer of the annual U.S. Open Championship.

Youngest British Ladies' champion Miss May Hezlet, a member of a famous Irish golfing family, was 17 when she won the first British Ladies' Championship at Newcastle, County Down.

Youngest British Open champion Tom Morris, Jr, was 18 when he won the championship at Prestwick in 1868.

Youngest U.S. Amateur champion Robert Gardner at 19 years 5 months won in 1909 at Chicago.

Youngest U.S. Ladies' champion Miss Beatrice Hoyt, 16, won the title at Morristown, New Jersey, in 1896.

Youngest U.S. Open champion Horace Rawlins, the first winner in 1895, was 19. He was only fractionally younger than John H. McDermott who won in 1912.

Youngest Walker Cup player   John Langley was 17 when he played for the British Isles team in the 1936 match at Pine Valley.

FAMOUS FIGURES IN THE GAME

Alliss, Percy   One of Britain's outstanding professionals between the wars. Born at Sheffield in 1897, he spent several years as a professional in Berlin but returned to England and played in four Ryder Cup matches. He died in 1975.

Alliss, Peter   Younger son of Percy Alliss, he had an even better record than his father in the Ryder Cup series, playing seven times from 1953 to 1967. Born in Berlin in 1931, he was a boy international at 15 but soon afterwards turned professional. Now well-known T.V. commentator.

Armour, Tommy   A distinguished Scots amateur who went to the United States and became a famous professional. He was born in Edinburgh in 1896, and he died in 1968. Apart from winning the United States Open Championship in 1927 and the British Open Championship in 1931, he was unique in as much as he played for Britain against the United States as an amateur and for the United States against Britain as a professional.

Auchterlonie, William   One of a long line of St Andrews club-makers, he was born there in 1872 and won the Open Championship in 1893. He was professional to the Royal and Ancient from 1935 till his death.

Ball, John   Born Hoylake, Cheshire, 1861. He first played in the Open Championship at 15 and finished eighth. The Amateur Championship did not begin until 1885, but between 1888 and 1912 he won the title eight times. In 1890 he became the first amateur ever to win the Open Championship. He made his last appearance in the Amateur Championship in 1921 at the age of 64 when he reached the sixth round. Doubtless the fact that he served in the Boer War and World War I prevented him from winning more championships. He died in December, 1940.

Barton, Pamela   One of the great women golfers between the wars, she equalled a 27-year-old record in 1936 when she won the British and American titles in the same season. She was only 19 at the time but a promising career was cut short by her death in an air crash in 1943 while serving in the W.A.A.F.

Beharrell, John Youngest ever winner of the British Amateur Championship being 18 when he won in 1956. Ten years later the South African, Bobby Cole, won the championship at the same age as Beharrell to the day.

Bonallack, Angela (*née* Ward) First came into prominence by winning the Kent championship in 1955. Three years later, shortly after her marriage to Michael Bonallack, she became English champion and went on to enjoy a successful career parallel with that of her husband.

Bonallack, Michael The greatest British amateur of his generation, he crowned a magnificent career in 1971 when he led Britain to a thrilling victory in the Walker Cup match at St Andrews. Born in 1934 at Chigwell, Essex, he won the Boys' Championship in 1952 and nine years later scored the first of five victories in the British Amateur Championship. He also won the English Amateur title and the *Golf Illustrated* Gold Vase five times, the British Stroke Play Championship twice, and many other competitions. He won the Amateur crown three times running (1968–70).

Bradshaw, Harry One of Ireland's most famous golfers. Lost the British Open Championship after a play-off with Bobby Locke at St George's in 1949. There might not have been a play-off if his ball had not lodged in a broken bottle earlier in the Championship, from which position he played it with disastrous results. He was born in 1913.

Braid, James Five times British Open champion, Braid was born at Elie, Fife, in 1870 and died in 1950, having been professional at Walton Heath, Surrey, for 45 years. He was a joiner by trade and played as an artisan amateur till 1893 when he became a club-maker in London. He scored all his Open wins in the ten years from 1901 to 1910 and in the same period was runner-up three times, in addition to winning the P.G.A. Match Play Championship three times. A tall, strong man, noted for his furious hitting, yet possessing a remarkably equable temperament; he spoke little but always to the point and was greatly respected by all who knew him. With Vardon and Taylor he formed the GREAT TRIUMVIRATE, three great professionals who dominated the golfing scene from 1894 to 1914.

Brown, Eric Chalmers   One of the first British amateurs to turn professional in maturity, doing so at the age of 21 after winning the Scottish Amateur title. He represented Great Britain in Ryder Cup matches on five occasions, the last as non-playing captain in 1971, and played eleven times for Scotland in the Canada (now World) Cup. He was twice Match Play champion and won the Vardon Trophy in 1957. He was born in Edinburgh in 1925.

Bruen, James   A youthful prodigy known far and wide for a loop at the top of his swing which defied analysis but seemed to increase rather than impair the power of his driving. He first became prominent as a 16-year-old winner of the Boys' Amateur Championship at Birkdale, beating his opponent by 11 and 9 in the final. Ten years later, on the same course, he won the British Amateur Championship. In 1939 he finished first amateur in the British Open after leading the qualifiers. Born in 1920, Bruen was only 18 when he helped to win the Walker Cup for Britain at St Andrews.

Campbell, Miss Dorothy (later Mrs D. C. Hurd)   Born at Edinburgh in 1883, she achieved a record by winning the British and American championships in the same year, 1909. She also won the Canadian Championship three times and is the only British golfer to have held all three titles.

Carr, Joseph B.   Without doubt the greatest amateur ever produced by Ireland, and one of the outstanding world amateurs in the post-war decade from 1947. His record overlapped that of Michael Bonallack, for he played in every Walker Cup match from 1947 to 1963 and was non-playing captain in 1967. He was practically unbeatable in Ireland for all that time and played for 21 years in the Irish international team. Born in 1922, he won the British Amateur title three times, his first victory being gained in a thrilling final at Hoylake in 1953, when he beat Harvie Ward, American holder of the title, on the home green. In 1971 he saw his son Roddy follow as a Walker Cup player and help to win the Cup for Britain at St Andrews. Roddy is now a professional.

Charles, Robert J.   Only 27 when he won the British Open Championship at Lytham, after a play-off with American Phil

Rodgers. Born in New Zealand in 1936, he became New Zealand Open champion at 18 and during the next ten years established himself as the greatest left-handed player in history. A great stylist and a wonderful putter, he had a record round of 66 in the 1963 British Open which included only 26 putts. In the 1968 British Open he tied for second place, one stroke behind Gary Player, and in 1969 was runner-up to Tony Jacklin.

Coles, Neil A consistent golfer, he has won almost every important British event except the British Open Championship. London-born in 1934, he has played in every Ryder Cup match against the United States since 1961, and has been British Match Play champion twice, in 1964 and 1965. Won Dunlop Masters, 1966. (Pl. 5.) and P.G.A. Championship, 1976.

Colt, H. S. Scratch golfer and famous course designer. Born in London in 1875. First secretary of the Sunningdale Golf Club, formed in 1901, he completed the design of Sunningdale Old Course and subsequently embarked on a career as golf architect which often took him to the United States.

Corcoran, Fred The first impresario of golf, he set the fashion for the sophisticated and expert management so evident today. Born in Massachusetts in 1909, he was an early manager for Walter Hagen and in 1937 became tournament manager for the U.S.P.G.A., and was appointed manager of the U.S. Ryder Cup team. After World War II he founded and managed the U.S. Ladies' P.G.A. Later he helped to start the Canada (now World) Cup and is tournament director of the International Golf Association, which controls that event.

Cotton, Thomas Henry, M.B.E. The greatest British professional since Vardon. He won many tournaments and honours, including three British Open championships, in a playing career of nearly 40 years. Born in 1907, he turned professional at 17, became a full professional before he was 20, was Open champion at 27 and in 1958, aged 51, finished eighth in the Open. His first Open win in 1934 was historic because it followed ten successive American victories. He won again in 1937 and 1948. He became an established golf-course architect, and created many modern lay-outs in Britain and abroad, including the Penina Hotel course in Portugal.

Croome, Arthur C. M.   Born in 1866, he was a co-founder and first secretary of the Oxford and Cambridge Golfing Society.

Daly, Fred   An Ulsterman born at Portrush in 1911, who played in four Ryder Cup matches. He won the Open Championship in 1947 and was three times P.G.A. Match Play champion. He became assistant professional at Royal Portrush at 16 and at 17 was appointed full professional at Mahee, later starting his long association with the Balmoral Club in Belfast. Daly's best period was in the decade after the war, for following his Open win, he was runner-up to Cotton in 1948 and three times afterwards finished in the first four.

Darwin, Bernard   Born in 1876 at Downe, Kent, a grandson of the great Charles Darwin. He played three times for Cambridge University and several times for England, as well as taking part in the first Walker Cup match in 1922. He died in 1961.

Davies, John   Born in London in 1948, he is an outstanding amateur, having represented England, and Great Britain and Ireland, in numerous international matches, including the Walker Cup, Eisenhower Trophy, G.B. v. Europe, and England home internationals. He was a member of the European team to tour South Africa in 1974. He came close to the coveted Amateur title in 1976, when he was defeated by America's Dick Siderowf at the 37th hole at St Andrews. Davies is regarded as a professional amateur and is a member of a number of golf clubs.

Doleman, William   The most successful of four Musselburgh brothers who all achieved eminence as amateurs. Born in 1838, he was first amateur in the Open Championship eleven times from 1865 to 1884.

Duncan, George   A policeman's son from Aberdeen, he might have made a name as a footballer but became a professional golfer when 17 and had a distinguished career, which included victory in the 1920 Open Championship, three appearances in Ryder Cup matches, and numerous tournament wins. He was born in 1883, and in 1929, at the age of 46, captained the winning British Ryder Cup team at Moortown, Leeds, where he beat the American captain, Walter Hagen by 10 and 8 over 36 holes. He died in 1964.

Evans, Charles ('Chick')   One of the finest of all United States amateurs. He was born in 1890 and his successes included the United States Open Championship in 1916, after having been runner-up two years before, and the United States Amateur Championship in 1916 and 1920. Played for the United States against Britain five times.

Faulkner, Maximilian   Born at Bexhill, Sussex, in 1916, son of a professional, Max Faulkner's promising early career was interrupted by the war, in which he served in the R.A.F. He was fourth in the Open Championship in 1949, fourth again in 1950, and won the title at Portrush in 1951. He played in five Ryder Cup matches and won the P.G.A. Match Play title in 1953, the year he became British Senior champion.

Fry, Sidney Herbert   Born in 1869, he played several times for England and was runner-up in the 1902 Amateur Championship. He also won the Amateur Billiards Championship on a number of occasions and, not surprisingly, was renowned for his skill at putting.

Gourlay, John   The doyen of the feather-ball makers who worked in Scotland 150 years ago. He had a large business at Musselburgh and turned out more balls than any other producer.

Graham, John, Jr.   Born at Liverpool in 1887 he was a near contemporary and strong rival of John Ball and Harold Hilton, was rated about as good a golfer, yet the highest honours always eluded him. He was plus 5 at Hoylake, played for Scotland, and was five times in the Amateur Championship semi-finals without once winning the title.

Hagen, Walter, C.   The legendary showman of golf was born in Rochester, N.Y. in 1892. As a professional he won the U.S. Open Championship when 22 and took that title again in 1919. In the next ten years he won the British Open four times. He also played in six Ryder Cup matches, won many tournaments, and figured in a number of challenge matches. He beat Bobby Jones over 72 holes by 12 and 11, and lost to Archie Compston by 18 and 17 over the same distance. Within a week or two of his defeat by Compston he won the British Open for the third time. Hagen was a flamboyant and therefore popular character.

Hamilton-Russell, Lady Margaret   As Lady Margaret Scott, she won the first three British Ladies' championships in 1893–4–5. A daughter of Lord Eldon, she was a sister of the Hon. Osmund, Michael and Denys Scott, all international golfers. Michael won the Amateur Championship at the age of 54.

Havers, Arthur   British Open champion in 1923. Played in five Ryder Cup matches against the United States. In 1924 he beat Bobby Jones in a challenge match by 2 and 1.

Herd, Alexander   A native of St Andrews, he was apprenticed to a plasterer but the call of golf was too insistent and he was soon challenging Vardon, Braid and Taylor. The challenge was unsuccessful until 1902 when Herd played with the untried and suspected rubber-core ball, just then introduced, and won the Open at Hoylake. Born in 1868, he spent most of his career in England and was attached to the Moor Park Club until his death in 1944.

Hilton, Harold Horsfall   The only British amateur to win the Open Championship twice, which he did in 1892 and 1897. He was born at West Kirby, Cheshire, in 1869 and was a lifelong rival at Hoylake of John Ball. Hilton was also four times Amateur champion. He turned to golf journalism and was for many years Editor of *Golf Illustrated.*

Hogan, Ben W.   One of the outstanding figures of modern golf, partly because of his calculating, clinical methods which yielded such impressive results in his prime, and partly because of the aura associated with his remarkable escape from death in a car crash and his triumphant return to full power when everyone thought his golfing days were finished. Born at Dublin, Texas, in 1912, he became a professional at 17, but was 33 before he began to make his name. In four years—1945–8—he became world famous. He was top money winner in the U.S.A. three years running and in 1948 won the U.S. Open. His car accident occurred in 1949 but a year later he returned to golf, and won the U.S. Open again. He scored further wins in that event in 1951 and 1953, the year that he brilliantly won the British Open by four strokes at the first attempt at Carnoustie.

Huggett, Brian   Born in Porthcawl, Wales, in 1936, he is one of the most consistent of modern British golfers with many tournament successes. Played for Britain in Ryder Cup matches against the United States in 1963, 1967, 1969, 1971, 1973. He won the British Match Play Championship in 1968 and the Dunlop Masters in 1970.

Hunt, Bernard   Captain of the 1973 British Ryder Cup team against the United States. Before 1973 he played in eight Ryder Cup matches; the only ones he has missed since 1953 were those of 1955 and 1971. Non playing Captain 1973. Won German Open Championship in 1961, the Belgian in 1957, French Open Championship in 1967 and the Dunlop Masters in 1965–67. Born Atherstone, 1930.

Hutcheon, Ian   A distinguished Scottish amateur, born in Monifieth, Angus, in 1942. He is a true amateur in the real sense of the word, and a telephone engineer by profession. As a member of the team that won the 1976 Eisenhower Trophy, he was the joint individual winner and anchor man to the side. He has won his country's Amateur Championship and Stroke-Play titles. Apart from playing in the Walker Cup, he has represented Great Britain and Ireland, and Scotland. He excels in both stroke and match-play golf.

Hutchinson, Horace G.   One of the earliest writers on golf, he was an all-round athlete who played golf, cricket, rugger and soccer for Oxford, and also rowed, played billiards and won prizes at athletics and swimming. Born in London in 1859, he spent his early life at Westward Ho! and was concerned as a schoolboy with the start of the North Devon Golf Club, of which his father was a founder member. By winning the scratch medal, Horace became the club captain at 16. Twice Amateur champion, a founder member of the Oxford University Golf Club, and a captain of the Royal and Ancient.

Hutchison, Jock   Born in 1884 at St Andrews, Scotland, where he won the British Open Championship in 1921 after a tie with the British Amateur, Roger Wethered. He won the United States Professional Golfers' Championship three times.

Irwin, Hale   An American professional born in 1945, who became a figurehead when he won the U.S. Open in 1974. From that point he has gone on from strength to strength to be a consistent and, some might say, a mechanical golfer. He will always be associated with the now discontinued Piccadilly World Match-Play Championship, in which, in the historic

1976 final, he was defeated at the 38th hole by the superhuman putting of Australia's David Graham.

Jacklin, Anthony The lorry driver's son who became the wealthiest professional in Britain in less than ten years. Born at Scunthorpe, Lincolnshire, in 1944, he turned professional at 18, and seven years later won the British Open at Lytham, being the first home player to do so for 18 years. In 1965 he won the Assistants' Championship and began his quick surge to the top. At 22 he represented England in the Canada (now World) Cup tournament, and a year later became a Ryder Cup player. In 1968 he went to the United States and won the Jacksonville Open Tournament, and in 1970, while still holding the British title, he astonished the world by winning the U.S. Open by seven strokes. (Pl. 3.)

Jones, Robert Tyre, Jr Acknowledged the greatest amateur golfer of all time. He died in 1971, aged 69. The highspot of a short but brilliant career came in 1930 when, aged only 28, he set up a record by winning the Open and Amateur championships of Britain and America in the same season. After that he retired from big golf, having won 13 national titles in seven years, including three British Open and four American Opens. In addition he played in five Walker Cup matches, winning all his single games and four of the five foursomes. He helped to start the U.S. Masters tournament in Augusta in his home state of Georgia, and on his last public appearance in Britain, in 1958, he captained the American team in the first Eisenhower Trophy tournament and was made a Freeman of St Andrews.

Kirkaldy, Andrew A notable figure in St Andrews golf for many years, he served as professional to the Royal and Ancient from 1904 till his death in 1934. Born in 1860, he became such a good golfer in his teens that he was runner-up in the 1879 Open Championship. But almost immediately afterwards he joined the Army, serving eight years with the Highland Light Infantry and seeing action in the Sudan campaign. On returning to civil life he soon became prominent in golf again and was twice more runner-up for the Open.

Laidlay, John E. One of the most distinguished members of the Honourable Company of Edinburgh Golfers. Born in 1860, he won more than 130 scratch medals, including the principal Royal and Ancient awards, and was twice Amateur champion.

Leitch, Miss Cecilia Pitcairn Known always as Cecil Leitch, she was one of the finest women golfers of all time. Born at Silloth, Cumberland, she played in the British Ladies' Amateur Championship at St Andrews in 1908, aged 15, and reached the semi-final. She won the title four times from 1914 to 1926.

Lema, Tony Born in 1934, Lema, an American, died with his wife in an aircraft accident in 1966. In 1964 he came to St Andrews and without a proper practice round, took the British Open Championship at the first attempt. Known as 'Champagne Tony', because after each success he presented a case of champagne to the Press.

Locke, Arthur d'Arcy (Bobby) South Africa's first great home-born golfer, he became famous in his own country at 17 when he won the South African Open and Amateur championships within a few days. A year later, in 1936, he paid his first visit to Britain and finished leading amateur in the Open. He turned professional in 1938 and, after wartime service as a bomber pilot with the South African Air Force, began the most rewarding part of his career. He won the British Open four times in addition to many big tournaments, and often finished top money winner. In 1946 and again in 1947 he played in the U.S. circuit and in the latter year finished second highest money winner. Locke was born in the Transvaal in 1917.

Longhurst, Henry Carpenter Born in Bedford, 1909. Leading golf correspondent and known on both sides of the Atlantic as a television golf reporter. Former captain of Cambridge University and former German Amateur champion.

Low, John Laing One of the 'fathers' of modern golf and principal architect of the rules. Born in Perthshire in 1869, he learned his golf at St Andrews. He also played soccer and lawn tennis, and was an Oxford Blue and Scottish International. He was first president of the Oxford and Cambridge Golfing Society and presented the President's Putter which is played for by the society each January at Rye, Sussex.

Lucas, Percy Belgrave Generally known as 'Laddie', he played in three Walker Cup matches against the United States and has won many amateur trophies. The best left-handed golfer Britain has so far produced. Lucas first became prominent in 1933 when he won the British Boys' Championship. He was born in 1915 and served with distinction as a fighter pilot in World War II.

Macfie, Allan Fullerton   Retains a rare place in golf history because although known as the first winner of the British Amateur Championship, he was not acknowledged as such until 34 years after winning the title. A native of St Andrews and a scratch player, he took part in an open amateur tournament organized by the Liverpool (later Royal) Golf Club in 1885 at Hoylake. This led to the institution of the Amateur Championship in 1886 and in 1919 MacFie's victory was officially recorded for the first time.

Massy, Arnaud   A sturdy Frenchman from the Basque area, he was the first overseas winner of the British Open Championship. He took the title at Hoylake in 1907 and promptly named his new daughter Hoylake!

Melville, Leslie M. Balfour   Amateur champion in 1895, he played for Scotland at golf, cricket, lawn tennis and rugger. Born in Edinburgh in 1854, he was captain of both the Royal and Ancient and the Honourable Company of Edinburgh Golfers.

Micklem, Gerald   Born Surrey 1911, he was English Amateur champion, 1947, 1953. Played in four Walker Cup matches against the United States, and many times for England. He was captain of the Royal and Ancient Club 1968–69.

Miller, Johnny   Californian born in 1947, he turned professional in 1969, and made a name for himself by winning the U.S. Open in 1973. He kept up a consistent form in 1974, his first 23 rounds being level par or better. He topped Jack Nicklaus' single season money winning record that year by more than $30,000 with his $353,021 and, in addition to his eight victories, he was placed in the top six in four other events. He is a practising Mormon and donates 10% of his winnings to his church.

Mitchell, Abe   A Sussex artisan golfer, he was unrivalled as an exponent of the game but seemed to lack the temperament for the big occasion. Born in 1887, he turned professional in 1913 after reaching the final of the British Amateur Championship, and after the war won a Victory tournament at St Andrews. This made him a favourite for the first post-war Open at Sandwich in 1920, and he led by six strokes after 36 holes. But he collapsed with a third round of 84 and the title went to George Duncan.

Morris, Tom (Called 'Old Tom' to distinguish him from his famous son.) He won the Open Championship four times from 1861 to 1867 and was associated with Allan Robertson in money matches. He also played many matches against Willie Park, his great rival. Morris was born at St Andrews in 1821 and died there in 1908, after having been professional to the Royal and Ancient for nearly 40 years. The home green of the Old Course is named after him.

Morris, Tommy Son of 'Old Tom', he was a golfer of such superlative skill and power that no one could stand against him during the lamentably short time he was in the game. Born at St Andrews in 1850, he won a major tournament when 16 and a year later won the Open Championship for the first time. He scored two more victories to win the original Belt outright, and won the first competition for the present Cup, to gain a fourth successive win—a record still unequalled. He was a fine man and a great golfer but his brilliant career was tragically cut short by his death at 25.

Nagle, Kel Born Australia 1920, Nagle reached the top comparatively late in life. His most famous performance was winning the Centenary British Open Championship at St Andrews in 1960. He was runner-up in 1962. He has been Australian, Canadian, French and New Zealand Open champion.

Nelson, John Byron So dominated his rivals in the United States during a successful decade that he became known as 'Mr Golf'. Born in Texas in 1912, he won the U.S. Open in 1939 and from 1942–5 was top money winner in the United States for four successive years. Ill-health forced a retirement from regular tournament play, but in 1946 he tied for the U.S. Open, losing in the play-off, and in 1947 made his third appearance in the Ryder Cup match.

Nicklaus, Jack William Following the modern trend, Nicklaus made his name first as an amateur and then turned professional. Born in 1940, he won the U.S. Amateur title twice, in 1959 and 1961, and in both those years played in the

(*above*) Mr Samuel Ryder (*left*), who donated the Ryder Cup for competition between members of the American P.G.A. and the British P.G.A., presenting the trophy to the British captain, George Duncan, after Britain's win at Moortown, Leeds, in 1929. (*right*) The great American, Ben Hogan (*left*) being presented with the Ryder Cup by Lord Wardington after Hogan had captained the American team to victory at Ganton in 1949

(*above*) In 1938 Henry Cotton played three great women golfers in a charity match at Maylands, Essex. *Left to right*: Miss Enid Wilson, Mme Rene Lacoste, Lady Heathcoat Amory and Henry Cotton. (*below*) John Ball of Hoylake was the greatest golfer of his day. He won the British Amateur Championship eight times and the British Open Championship once

COTTON T H 294

CERDA A

KING S L

VA DONCK F

(*above*) Bobby Locke
of South Africa
(*left*), four times
winner of the British
Open Championship,
receives the trophy
from the captain of the
Royal Lytham and St
Annes Club, Mr
Edward Lee, after his
victory in 1952. (*right*)
Mrs George Zaharias
('The Babe'),
America's greatest
woman golfer. She
won the British and
American Cham-
pionships before tur-
ning professional.
Photo shows her with
the British trophy at
Gullane in 1947

Walker Cup, winning his single and foursome on each occasion. He began his professional career by winning the U.S. Open in 1962, and this initiated a sequence of great performances which made him, by the end of 1972, the biggest money winner of all time. His winnings then amounted to $1,477,200.86. Nicklaus won the U.S. Open again in 1967 and 1971, and the British Open in 1966 and 1970.

O'Connor, Christy   An Irishman who came into prominence in 1955 when, on only his second visit to Great Britain, he won the first ever £1000 prize given in Britain. During the next 25 years he won many other big prizes, culminating in £25,000 as winner of the John Player Classic in 1970. Born in Donegal in 1925, he won the Canada (now World) Cup for Ireland in 1958 with Harry Bradshaw, played in five Ryder Cup matches for Britain, was twice Master Golfer (title of winner of the Dunlop Master tournament), twice leader of the season's averages, and once P.G.A. Match Play champion.

Oosterhuis, Peter A.   After a brilliant and precocious career as an amateur, he turned professional in 1970 and rapidly made his mark. In 1971 and again in 1972 Oosterhuis, who is British but of Dutch ancestry, won the Harry Vardon Trophy as leader of the Order of Merit, and played prominently in the Open Championship. Born in 1948, he was still at his public school when selected for the 1967 Walker Cup match, having already played for England. He won practically everything in the amateur field except a national title, and at 23, when he played in the Ryder Cup match was already regarded as a prodigy. Won Vardon Trophy 1971–2, 73–4. (Pl. 7.)

Ouimet, Francis D.   A famous American player and legislator, he had the distinction in 1913, when only 20 and virtually unknown, of tying with Harry Vardon and Ted Ray for the U.S. Open title and beating both British professionals in the play-off. Born in 1893, Ouimet became one of the elders of American golf after being involved in 12 Walker Cup matches, eight as a player and four as captain. He was elected captain of the Royal and Ancient club in 1951, the first American to be so honoured.

Palmer, Arnold   Son of a professional, he was only 23 when he won the U.S. Amateur Championship. He almost immediately turned professional to begin a decade of outstanding successes which made him the biggest prize-money winner of his day. Born in 1929, he won the Canadian Open at 25, became U.S. Open champion at 30, and in each of the next two years, 1961 and 1962, won the British Open. A phenomenally powerful driver with a very distinctive style, he also had a charming personality which helped to create an Arnold Palmer cult. This took tangible shape in 'Arnie's Army', the masses of golf fans who trooped along with him during his many triumphs.

Park, Willie, Sr   One of the great players of money matches in early Victorian times and a contemporary and constant rival of Tom Morris. Park beat Morris in the first Open Championship in 1860 and won on three later occasions. He was a tall, dignified man, like Morris, a cut above the average professional of those days.

Park, Willie, Jr   Son of the first Open champion, and himself winner of the title twice, in 1887 and 1889. He was beaten by one stroke by Harry Vardon in 1898. Born at Musselburgh in 1864, the younger Park was the first businessman professional and the first scientific golf-course designer. He laid out many fine courses at home and abroad. He died in 1925.

Pearson, Miss Isette (later Mrs T. H. Miller)   The first secretary of the Ladies' Golf Union, she helped to found the British Ladies' Amateur Championship in 1893, being runner-up to Lady Margaret Scott in each of the first two years.

Philip, Hugh   Acknowledged to have been the greatest of the old club-makers. He flourished at St Andrews nearly two centuries ago and was famous for his wooden-headed putters.

Player, Gary   Born in South Africa in 1935, the year when Bobby Locke, then aged 17, began his championship career. Twenty-four years later Player, now an accomplished performer, won the British Open. Unlike Locke, he rarely played in Britain but concentrated with great success on the American circuit and played in many other countries. In 1965 he became the first foreign golfer to win the U.S. Open since Britain's Ted Ray in 1920. Player won the British Open again in 1968 and in 1974 and has won many other honours including three victories in the Piccadilly World Match Play Championship.

Ray, Edward   A big, clumsy-looking man of tremendous power who, like his contemporary Harry Vardon, was a Channel

Islander, having been born in Jersey in 1877. Ray was a real character, always portrayed wearing a battered felt hat and puffing on a pipe which rarely left his mouth even while making a stroke. He won the British Open Championship in 1912 and the U.S. Open in 1920, and later played in the early Ryder Cup matches which he captained in 1926.

Rees, David James, C.B.E.   His playing career has extended over more than 40 years during which he won nearly 40 major tournaments and titles and secured many international honours. Born in 1913 in Wales, the son of a professional, he was only 23 when he won the P.G.A. Match Play Championship for the first of four times. He was also four times runner-up. He played in nine Ryder Cup matches which he captained on four occasions, including the 1957 match which Britain won. He was also non-playing captain in 1967.

Robertson, Allan   The first of the great 19th century professionals, and reputed unbeaten in single combat on level terms. He had a flourishing ball-making business at St Andrews where he was born in 1815. Both partner and rival of Tom Morris, Robertson died in 1858.

Roe, Commdr Robert Charles Thornber, R.N. (Ret.)
Secretary of the Professional Golfers' Association from 1934 to 1962. He died in 1976.

Rolland, Douglas   A native of the little Scots golfing town of Elie, Rolland soon established a local reputation and when the great John Ball at the height of his power challenged any amateur in the world, Rolland accepted and won handsomely.

Ryder, Samuel   A wealthy seed merchant, who showed great interest in the welfare of British golf. He appointed Abe Mitchell as his private professional in the hope, unfulfilled, that Mitchell, relieved of club responsibilities, would win the Open Championship. In 1927 he presented the Ryder Cup, now played for biennially between the United States and Great Britain. Ryder died in 1936 aged 77.

Sarazen, Eugene (Gene)   Only 20 when he won the U.S. Open Championship in 1922; ten years later he won that title and the British Open in the same season. Sarazen won the U.S. Masters in 1935 and played in six Ryder Cup matches.

Sayers, Bernard   'Wee Ben', as he was known, never won the Open Championship although he played in that event for more than 40 years. But he was a fine player, despite his small stature and slight build. He was born at Leith in 1857 and later settled at North Berwick where he established a flourishing club-making business which was carried on by his descendants after his death in 1924.

Smith, Mrs Frances (*née* Stephens)   Played in six Curtis Cup matches, in one of which, at Sandwich, in 1956, she made the winning stroke at the last hole of the deciding single to score Britain's second win in 23 years. She captained the side in 1962. Her individual record was most impressive—twice British champion, three times English champion, ten times Lancashire champion.

Smith, Macdonald   One of the great army of Carnoustie golfers who sought renown as professionals in the United States and elsewhere. He is considered an unlucky player for although he finished well up in the British Open Championship, he never won the event. In 1925 at Prestwick he went into the last round five strokes ahead but was engulfed by thousands of his admirers, who in the end were the cause of his losing the title they so much wanted him to win. He was born in 1890 and died when 59.

Snead, Samuel Jackson   Possessed one of the finest golf swings in the world, and he used it, with his wonderful temperament, to win practically every honour in the game except the Open Championship of his own country, the United States. Born in Virginia in 1912, he turned professional at 22, and three years later stormed into the tournament circuit. He took generous pickings for the next 30 years, winning the British Open in 1946, the U.S. Masters three times, the United States P.G.A. Championship three times and the Canada (now World) Cup three times, paired in turn with Ben Hogan, Arnold Palmer and Jimmy Demaret.

Tait, Frederick Guthrie   Twice British Amateur champion and one of the finest golfers ever produced by Scotland, he had a tragically short life. Born in Edinburgh in 1870, he went to South Africa with his regiment, the Black Watch, and was killed in action in 1900.

Taylor, John Henry With Vardon and Braid he formed the GREAT TRIUMVIRATE who between them won the Open 16 times in 21 years. Taylor's share was five wins, the first being in 1894 when he was the first non-Scottish professional to hold the title. Born at Northam, North Devon, in 1871, he soon became involved in golf as a caddie on the Royal North Devon links at Westward Ho! where many years later he became the club's president. He spent most of his professional career with the Royal Mid-Surrey Club at Richmond and died in retirement, at Northam, in his 92nd year.

Thomson, Peter W., M.B.E. Made history at Birkdale in 1965 when he joined J. H. Taylor and James Braid as five times winner of the Open Championship. Born at Melbourne in 1929, he first became prominent in 1948 as leading amateur in the Australian Open Championship. He turned professional the following year, aged 20, and scored many successes in Australia, New Zealand, and especially Britain. (Pl. 2.)

Tolley, Cyril James Hastings, M.C. Immediately after serving in World War I he went to Oxford University, and in 1920, at Muirfield, beat the American, Bob Gardner, at the 37th hole of the British Amateur Championship final. He won the title again in 1929. Tolley was born in 1895 and played in six Walker Cup matches.

Travis, Walter An Australian who made his home in the United States. Won the United States Amateur Championship three times and caused a sensation by winning the British Amateur Championship in 1904 using a centre-shafted putter which was banned in Britain for many years afterwards. Travis was something of an eccentric who made a great impact on American golf. Born in Australia in 1862, he died in New York in 1927.

Vardon, Harry The greatest golfer of his generation, his record of six victories in the British Open Championship seems now to be unassailable. His style and methods were imitated all over the world as models of what a golf swing should be, and by a very successful tour of the United States in 1900 he exerted a great and lasting influence on American golf. Born at Grouville, Jersey, in 1870, a few months after Braid and ten months before Taylor, he spent his career in friendly rivalry with both these men, and the three of them were known in the golfing world as the 'great triumvirate'. He set the seal on his fame in 1914 at Prestwick by tying with Taylor and winning the play-off, to score his sixth Open win. Vardon died in 1937 after spending most of his life as professional to the South Herts Club at Totteridge.

Vicenzo, Roberto de   The best of several fine golfers from South America, he had many successes in a number of countries before reaching the climax of his career by winning the British Open Championship at Hoylake in 1967. He was born in Buenos Aires in 1923.

Wethered, Joyce (later Lady Heathcoat-Amory)   Miss Wethered became prominent immediately after World War I, first as partner to her brother, Roger Wethered, and then in her own right when she beat Cecil Leitch, then the acknowledged queen of British golf, in the English Championship. She won that title five times running and during the same period was three times British champion. She virtually gave up golf in 1925 but returned for the British Championship of 1929 at St Andrews and beat the American, Glenna Collett (afterwards Mrs Vare) in the final, after being five down in the first round. She emerged again from private life to play in the first Curtis Cup match in 1932, and again in 1935 for a tour of the United States.

Wethered, Roger Henry   Played in the 1920–1 Oxford University teams with Cyril Tolley, and with Joyce Wethered formed a famous brother-and-sister partnership. In 1921 he tied for the Open Championship at St Andrews, losing to Jock Hutchison in the play-off. Two years later he won the Amateur Championship and went on to many more achievements, including five Walker Cup appearances. He was born in 1899 and was captain of the Royal and Ancient in 1946.

Whitcombe, Charles Albert   One of three famous brothers who all played in the Ryder Cup match although he made the most appearances—six—and was captain in 1931. He was born in 1895.

Whitcombe, Ernest R.   Oldest of the Whitcombe brothers, he was born in 1890 and played in several Ryder Cup matches. He only just failed to win the Open Championship in 1924, losing by one stroke to Walter Hagen.

Whitcombe, Reginald A. Youngest of the Whitcombe brothers, he had a less imposing record but for one high spot—he was the only one to win the Open Championship, which he did in a gale at Sandwich in 1938. He played in the Ryder Cup match only once, in 1935, when both his brothers were also in the team.

White, Jack A native of North Berwick, he graduated from local caddie to Open champion, and became a noted club-maker. Born in 1873, he was appointed professional to the newly opened Sunningdale Club in 1903, and in the following year won the Open Championship at Sandwich with a record low aggregate of 296.

Wilson, Enid Won the British women's championship three years running, 1931–3, played in the first Curtis Cup match in 1932, and had many other successes before turning to journalism. She was born at Stonebroom, Derbyshire in 1910.

Zaharias, Mrs George (*née* Mildred Didrikson) Known as 'The Babe', she was the pioneer of professional golf for women, and the greatest player of her time. She was an outstanding athlete and in 1932 won three Olympic field events with record figures. Taking up golf, she quickly mastered that game also, demonstrating the possession of immense power and determination. She won the U.S. Women's Amateur Championship in 1946 and after taking the British title at Gullane in 1947 turned professional. A distinguished career in that sphere ended with an illness and she died from cancer in 1956, aged 41.

FAMOUS BRITISH CLUBS
AND COURSES

Alnmouth, Alnmouth, Northumberland   The little-known Alnmouth Club in the north-east corner of England is one of the oldest golf clubs in England, having been formed in 1867, only three years after the now Royal North Devon Club at Westward Ho! Being near the border between England and Scotland it is likely that Alnmouth owes its early beginning to golfers from Scotland.

Blairgowrie, Rosemount, Blairgowrie   Founded in 1889, Rosemount has in recent years become increasingly popular as visiting golfers have realized its immense qualities. Not perhaps as spectacular as its comparatively near neighbour, Gleneagles, Rosemount has few equals in Britain as an inland course.

Bruntsfield Links Golfing Society, Davidson's Mains, Edinburgh   The society, it is claimed, dates back to 1761. Its links were once in Edinburgh and later the society shared the Musselburgh course with the Musselburgh Club and the Honourable Company of Edinburgh Golfers. It is also possible that the society had some connection with that body of golfers who became the Royal Burgess Golfing Society which claims an earlier date for its foundation.

Burnham and Berrow, Burnham-on-Sea, Somerset   The club was formed in 1890 and has been the scene of many championship events. It is a typical seaside links and within its boundaries is a church still used as a place of worship on Sundays.

Carnoustie, Carnoustie, Angus   This is one of the great Scottish public links and is on the rota for the British Open and Amateur championships. Golf was first played in the famous Scottish nursery in 1847 and since then it has supplied hundreds of professionals to other parts of the world. The greatest moment in the recent history of Carnoustie was when the great American player Ben Hogan won the British Open in 1953 to add to his U.S. title. The medal course can be stretched to more than 7200 yd (6584 m), the longest in Britain.

Crail Golfing Society, Crail, Fife   A very old club dating from 1786, situated a few miles to the south of St Andrews. For real natural golf this fine seaside course, of approximately 6000 yd (5486 m), is full of interest, being on one of the eastern-most points of Scotland.

Formby, Formby, Lancashire   Founded in 1884, this is one of the many well-cultured links along the Lancashire coastline. It has been the venue of the British Amateur Championship and is praised by all who have tackled its fine fairways and greens. Formby has its own annual amateur tournament, the Formby Hare.

Ganton, Ganton, Yorkshire   Only a few miles from the famous seaside resort of Scarborough, Ganton, founded in 1891, is a compact championship circuit which has had the honour of staging a Ryder Cup contest, and the British Amateur Championship.

Glasgow, Bearsden, Glasgow   The Glasgow Club goes back to 1787. It has two courses, one actually in Glasgow at Killermont and one on the Ayrshire coast at Gailes. The two courses are very different in character, Killermont being a parkland course set round a big mansion-type club-house, while Gailes is a typical seaside course.

Gleneagles, Gleneagles, Perthshire   If only for the sheer beauty of the scenic view, golfers should visit Gleneagles. Founded in 1925, it has two 18-hole courses aptly named the Kings and Queens, and another under construction. It has staged the Curtis Cup golf match and other major events. The courses adjoin one of Britain's luxury hotels. There is also a club-house.

Gullane, Gullane, East Lothian   Founded in 1882, there are three courses at Gullane, all situated at the west end of the village, the opposite end to where one turns up the narrow lane to Muirfield. The village is only about ½ mile (0.8 km) long, but the three Gullane courses and Muirfield are entirely different, the Gullane ones being situated for the most part on Gullane Hill and all more of a downland character. Gullane No 1 is used as a qualifying test for the Open Championship and has also housed the British Ladies' Championship.

Hunstanton, Hunstanton, Norfolk   More than 80 years old, Hunstanton, founded in 1891, gives quality in its club-house facilities and links. It has been a popular venue for women's championships and there has been many an Oxford—Cambridge duel on this wind-battered stretch. It has also housed the English Amateur Championship.

Little Aston, Little Aston, Staffordshire   This is a fine parkland stretch, a mile or so away from the village of Streetly. It has character with variety at practically all its 18 holes. Founded in 1908, it has also had a full share of major events.

Montrose, Montrose, Angus   The date when golf was played on the stretch of links in the Angus coast town is in doubt, but it is known that the great Scottish nobleman, the Marquess of Montrose, who died in 1650, was a keen golfer and that he played at Leith, St Andrews and Montrose, so it is reasonable to suppose that Montrose is one of the oldest golf links in Scotland. In the early days of the game and for long after it was known for the many famous golf-club makers who were natives of the town. It is a course shared between the public and four private clubs, the oldest being the Royal Albert Club which dates from 1810.

Moortown, Moortown, Leeds   Founded in 1908, Moortown on the Leeds—Harrogate road has been conspicuous throughout its history for many important events, including one of the early Ryder Cup matches.

Muirfield, Gullane, East Lothian   Home of the Honourable Company of Edinburgh Golfers who moved there from Musselburgh in 1891. It is now an up-to-date circuit for the big-time events such as the Open Championship and Ryder Cup. This course is, according to most golfers, the supreme test and in its compact stretch gives all spectators a fair view. (*See also* EDINBURGH GOLFERS, HONOURABLE COMPANY OF.)

Prestwick, Prestwick, Ayrshire   This club, which inaugurated the Open Championship in 1860, was founded nine years before, in 1851. The first twelve Open championships were held there and it has also housed nine Amateur championships. It is a typical seaside course with large bunkers and the inevitable stream, or 'burn'.

147

Royal Birkdale, Southport, Lancashire In 1889 eight enthusiasts set about transforming a rugged stretch of land into a course with a small wooden club-house. Then in the early thirties a modern club-house was built and Royal Birkdale (honoured with royal Patronage in 1951) broke through as a venue for practically every major event.

Royal Blackheath, Eltham, Kent Known to be in existence in 1766, it is the oldest club in England. As in the case of the Honourable Company of Edinburgh Golfers, a society existed before the formation of the club. It has been said that Royal Blackheath was instituted earlier, in 1608, but proof of this vanished in a fire at the end of the 18th century.

Royal Burgess Golfing Society of Edinburgh, Barnton, Edinburgh The club is situated just beyond the outskirts of Scotland's capital. It claims to be the oldest golf club in the world and that it was formed in 1735. Another date for its founding is given as 1773. Originally its members played over Leith Links and also at Musselburgh before moving to their present fine home at Barnton.

Royal Cinque Ports, Deal, Kent This natural seaside stretch is almost 80 years old and remains popular with various golfing societies. During 1909 and 1920 it housed Open championships and has also been the venue for the Amateur Championship. It is the permanent home of one of the biggest of British amateur golf events—the Public Schools Halford Hewitt competition. The club was founded in 1892.

Royal Liverpool, Hoylake, Cheshire Founded in 1869, this is a classic championship stretch on which many famous players, such as de Vicenzo, Player and Thomson, have performed. It has also been on the rota for Amateur championships and staged the first British Amateur Championship in 1885.

Royal Lytham and St Annes, St Annes, Lancashire Founded in 1886, Royal Lytham and St Annes links is one of the classic championship links. It can be extended to nearly 7000 yd (6400 m) and apart from its fame as hosts to Open championships it saw the first ever left-handed winner of a British Open in Bob Charles and Tony Jacklin's Open Championship victory in 1969.

148

Royal Mid-Surrey, Richmond, Surrey   Founded in 1892, the course was designed by J. H. Taylor who was the club professional for many years before Henry Cotton. A pleasant parkland course on which has been played such events as the English Amateur Championship and the British Boys' Championship.

Royal Musselburgh, Prestonpans, East Lothian   Founded in 1774, this is one of the oldest clubs and has the distinction of staging the Open championships between 1874 and 1889. The Honourable Company of Edinburgh Golfers moved to Musselburgh in 1836 where they shared the course with two other societies. In 1891, however, they decided to move to Muirfield. Musselburgh has unlimited history, including many stories of the famous Park family, among them Willie Park, winner of the Open Championship four times.

Royal Co. Down, Newcastle, County Down   One of Northern Ireland's oldest clubs, it was founded in 1889. It has a championship stretch of nearly 7000 yd (6400 m) and has been the venue of the British Amateur Championship and international matches.

Royal North Devon, Westward Ho!, Northam, Devon   Founded in 1864, this is the oldest English seaside course, and the oldest English club still playing on its original site. It is one year older than the London Scottish Club which still plays on Wimbledon Common. Westward Ho! has housed several championships. In the early days of golf it was renowned for its artisan golfers, many of whom, including J. H. Taylor, became famous professionals. The club played host to the Martini international in 1975.

Royal Perth Golfing Society, Perth   Founded in 1822, this club is the oldest 'royal' club of all, having been given royal patronage by King William IV in 1833. Perth holds an important place in golfing history, for the game has been played there since 1502 when King James IV was one of its devotees.

Royal Porthcawl, Porthcawl, Glamorganshire   Probably the best test for any golfer in Wales. It is on the coastline and provides a natural challenge—more so in the winds which blow in from the sea. It has been the venue of Amateur championships and staged the Curtis Cup of 1964.

Royal Portrush, Portrush, Co. Antrim   The seaside course of the Royal Portrush Club in Northern Ireland has many spectacular holes. The club was founded in 1888 and it has housed many important British and Irish events, including the British Open Championship in 1951 when it was won by Max Faulkner. The British Amateur Championship was played there in 1960 and the British Ladies' Championship has been played on the course seven times.

Royal St George's, Sandwich, Kent   At one time the venue of the Open Championship, Royal St George's is rated high among British courses. Apart from the Open it has tested golfers to the full in the Walker Cup international and the Penfold P.G.A. Championship. It was founded in 1887.

Royal St David, Harlech, Merionethshire   A fine old seaside course dating from 1894. It has been the home of all the important Welsh events, and the British Ladies' Championship has been played there on four occasions, in 1926, 1949, 1960 and 1967.

Royal Wimbledon, Wimbledon, London   Royal Wimbledon is an offshoot of the club founded by the London Scottish Rifle Volunteers regiment whose members were given permission to play golf on Wimbledon Common in 1865. The club became known as the London Scottish Golf Club. In 1880 some civilian golfers broke away to form their own club, on another part of the common, and this is the club known today as Royal Wimbledon. In 1908 Wimbledon Common Club was formed to share the original course with London Scottish, which they do even now. Each club has its own club-house. Players on this course must wear a red jacket, pullover or shirt so that the public walking on the Common are aware of the presence of golfers. This regulation does not apply to the Royal Wimbledon course. Royal Wimbledon did much for the game in the early days, having been concerned with the first general set of rules and also with the formation of the Ladies' Golf Union. (*See also* HISTORY OF GOLF, p. 14.)

Saunton, Braunton, North Devon   Situated across the estuary from its more famous neighbour, Westward Ho!, Saunton dates back to 1891, although the present course bears little resemblance to the earlier one. It is a typical seaside links, and the British Ladies' Championship was played there in 1932. It has also housed the English Amateur Championship.

Southport and Ainsdale, Southport, Lancashire   The Southport and Ainsdale club was formed in 1907. Although overshadowed to some extent by its famous near neighbours, Formby and Royal Birkdale, S. and A., as it is popularly called, is a great seaside links with some huge sandtraps. It was the scene of two Ryder Cup matches, in 1933 and 1937.

Sunningdale, Sunningdale, Berkshire   One of the most popular clubs near London. It has two courses, the Old and New, and is invariably packed during the summer with visiting societies. It has staged many important meetings including the Dunlop Masters, qualifying contests for the Open Championship, the *Golf Illustrated* Gold Vase tournament for top amateurs and the Colgate Women's European Championship. The club was founded in 1900.

St Andrews, St Andrews, Fife   The seaside town in Scotland generally referred to as the 'home of golf'. There are four courses at St Andrews: the Old, the New, the Eden and the Jubilee. The Royal and Ancient Club has its headquarters at St Andrews and there are two other famous clubs also in the town, the St Andrews Club and the New Club. There is also a famous ladies' club, St Rule's. Golf has been played at St Andrews since about 1550. The courses are administered by a local representative body.

Most of the great golf events have been staged at St Andrews from the Open Championship to the Walker Cup. (*See also* ROYAL AND ANCIENT CLUBS OF ST ANDREWS *and* Pls. 1 and 2.)

Troon, Troon, Ayrshire   Founded in 1878, Troon, with its Old Troon championship links, has been the scene of many Open Championships. Like St Andrews, it has other facilities on nearby courses and includes a popular municipal links. (Pls. 2 and 4.)

Turnberry, Turnberry, Ayrshire   One of Scotland's best coastline courses, two of them in fact—Arran and Ailsa. The Arran course is first class and has a marvellous scenic view. It has housed the *News of the World* Match Play Championship, the Walker Cup, the John Player Classic, and was the venue for the 1977 British Open. The club was founded in 1903.

Walton Heath, Walton Heath, Surrey   Founded in 1904, it had as one of its earliest professionals the famous James Braid.

A fine golfing stretch with two courses, the Old and New. It was for many years the home of the *News of the World* Match Play Championship. Now is venue for the *Golf Illustrated* Gold Vase.

Wentworth, Virginia Water, Surrey   One of the newest of the clubs near London, having been founded in 1924. There are two courses of 18 holes, the East and West, the latter more familiarly known as the 'Burma Road' because of a severe trek of nearly 7000 yd (6400 m). A popular choice among sponsors of professional events, it has housed the Ryder Cup, the Piccadilly World match play event and in 1977 saw the inauguration of the Colgate World Match Play Championship.

Woodhall Spa, Woodhall Spa, Lincolnshire   A golfing oasis set in the bleak fenland of Lincolnshire, Woodhall Spa is, according to many competent judges, the finest inland course in England. It could best be described as Heathland, but its layout, the work of Colonel Hotchkin who was its owner before his death, is of exceptional quality. The course is now owned by Mr Neil Hotchkin, Colonel Hotchkin's son, who in 1972 was President of the English Golf Union. Woodhall Spa dates back to 1905.

FAMOUS AMERICAN CLUBS

Augusta National, Augusta, Georgia One of the most famous of all American golf clubs. Founded in 1931, Augusta National Course was a dream come true for the great Robert Tyre Jones and his friend, Clifford Roberts. The professional architect engaged was Dr Mackenzie, ably advised by Jones. In 1934 the first Masters Tournament was held on the course and now it is one of the premier events on the golfing calendar. Entry for the tournament is by invitation. First winner of the Masters was Horton Smith. It was in the Masters in 1968 that the partner of Argentina's Roberto de Vicenzo wrongly marked Vicenzo's card and the Argentinian, who would have won, was disqualified.

Baltusrol, Springfield, New Jersey One of the oldest clubs in the United States, it was founded in 1895 and housed the first of its many championships, the Ladies' Championship, in 1901. Since then Baltusrol has housed all the premier American championships. There are now two courses, the tougher of the two being the Lower Course. The new courses were built in the early twenties.

Brae Burn, Brae Burn Country Club, West Newton, Mass. This old American club was founded in 1897. It housed the United States Open Championship in 1919 and the U.S. Amateur Championship in 1928. It was also the scene of the 1970 Women's Curtis match which ended in a tie.

Brookline Country Club, Brookline, Mass. The club dates back as far as golf is concerned to 1892 although other sporting activities were held there before then. There have been two dramatic U.S. Open championships at Brookline, that of 1913 when Francis Ouimet beat Harry Vardon and Ted Ray in a play-off, and in 1963 when Julius Boros beat Arnold Palmer and Billy Casper in a play-off. The club has also hosted the U.S. Amateur Championship, the U.S. Ladies' Championship and the 1932 Walker Cup match. Brookline was one of the founder members of the association which became the United States Golf Association.

Chicago, Chicago, Illinois   If John Reid was the 'father' of American golf, another of the pioneers was Charles Blair Macdonald, a young American who was educated at St Andrews, Scotland. He played golf on a rough piece of ground in Chicago in 1875, but there was no club. It was not until 1892 that he persuaded some enthusiasts to lay out a course at Lake Forest. He was given the task of designing the course which became the home of the Chicago Club. A 9-hole course was later laid out and this course became the home of the famous Onwentsia Club. In the early days of American golf, Chicago had 26 clubs, including one by the name of Westward Ho!

Inverness, Toledo, Ohio   This old American club is best remembered in Britain as being the club where the Englishman, Ted Ray, won the United States Open Championship in 1920. Ray's victory was a surprise but no greater a surprise than when the almost unknown Dick Mayer took the title there in 1957.

Merion, Merion Golf Club, Ardmore, Pa.   Strangely enough this club began life as Merion Cricket Club and staged its first important event, the U.S. Amateur Championship, in 1916 when one of the competitors was a 14-year-old named Robert Tyre Jones. In 1930 the winner was the same Robert Tyre Jones who that year won the 'Grand Slam': the U.S. Amateur and Open championships and the British Amateur and Open championships. It was also at Merion in 1950 that Ben Hogan made his great come-back after his car crash to win the Open Championship. Lee Trevino won the 1971 U.S. Open at Merion.

Minikahda, Minneapolis, Minnesota   The picturesque course of this famous club, founded in 1898, has seen the United States Open Championship and the Walker Cup match. Its Open Championship, that of 1916, is remembered as being won by an amateur, the famous Chick Evans. Bobby Jones won the 1927 U.S. Amateur Championship there.

Newport, Newport, Rhode Island   The club has a special place in American golf, for it was a founder member of the forerunner of the United States Golf Association, and it was on the Newport course that the first United States Open Championship and the first United States Amateur Championship was held in 1895. The club was started by Mr Theodore A. Havemeyer who became the first president of the national body which became the U.S. Golf Association.

Oakland Hills, Birmingham, Mich.   The Oakland Hills Country Club came into existence in 1918, and its course was planned by two famous golf-course architects. It was originally designed by Donald Ross and modernized in 1951 by Robert Trent Jones. Its first professional was Walter Hagen. It has housed the United States Open Championship on four occasions, in 1924, 1937, 1951 and 1961.

Oakmont, Oakmont, Pa.   Oakmont staged its first championship, the U.S. Amateur, in 1919 when Bobby Jones was the beaten finalist. Next time the event was held there in 1925, Jones won. Hogan won his last U.S. Open on this course in 1953 and the great Tommy Armour won his Open there in 1927, as did Jack Nicklaus in 1962.

Olympic, San Francisco, California   Originally Olympic was an athletic club, golf not being played in the club until much later on in its history. The 16th hole measures 604 yd (552 m) and is claimed to be the longest hole of any championship course. In 1955 Ben Hogan was beaten by Jack Fleck in a play-off for the U.S. Open at Olympic and in 1966 Billy Casper beat Arnold Palmer there in a play-off for the Open Championship. There are two courses at Olympic.

Pebble Beach, Pebble Beach, California. This must be one of the most photographed golf courses in the world. It is one of the most beautiful and exciting courses in the United States, yet although it has been the scene of professional events such as the U.S. Open, it has on the whole been neglected for championships. However, Jack Nicklaus won his last U.S. Amateur Championship there in 1961. It was the venue of the United States Open Championship in 1972.

Pinehurst, Pinehurst, North Carolina   This is one of the great golf centres in the United States, having five courses, the oldest being the championship course which was designed by Donald Ross in 1901. The 1962 U.S. Amateur Championship was played at Pinehurst, as was the 1951 Ryder Cup match. It housed the 1973 World Open Golf Championship with prize money of £200,000.

Portland, Portland, Oregon   In Britain at any rate Portland, Oregon, is best remembered as the course where the first Ryder Cup match after World War II was played through the generosity of a great man of golf, Robert Hudson. When it looked as if the match could not be held Mr Hudson genersouly paid the British bill.

Shinnecock Hills, Southampton, New York   The course dates back to 1891 and was the work of Willie Dunn. He had designed one at Biarritz in France when he was invited by three wealthy Americans, including Mr W. K. Vanderbilt, to plan a course in New York. He designed the Southampton lay-out and became the club's first professional.

St Andrews   The first American golf club, St Andrews was the brainchild of an emigrant Scot, John Reid, from Fife in Scotland. The first course was one of three holes laid out on Mr Reid's cow pasture. After one other change of venue, the golfers moved to an apple orchard and became known in golfing history as the 'Apple Tree Gang'. They had one more move before arriving at the present home of the club at Mount Hope, Westchester. (*See also* HISTORY OF AMERICAN GOLF, p. 20.)

Winged Foot, Mamaroneck, New York   This famous club, which has two courses, was founded in 1923. It has been the scene of the U.S. Amateur Championship, the U.S. Ladies' Championship and the Walker Cup match. The courses are testing and spectacular despite the fact that neither is long by modern standards. (Pl. 4.)

FAMOUS WORLD CLUBS

Australia

Royal Melbourne One of Australia's most distinguished clubs; it was formed in 1891. There are two 18-hole courses. Apart from housing Australian championships, it has been the venue of World Cup matches for both amateurs and professionals.

Royal Sydney Two years younger than the Royal Melbourne, this club has had two homes. A fairly long and testing course, it has housed all the Australian championships.

Belgium

Royal Antwerp The oldest club in Belgium, having been established in 1888. There are two courses, one of 18 holes, one of 9 holes. The venue of important Belgian events.

Royal Golf Club de Belgique Established 1906. The course is at Tervueren, about 9 miles (14.5 km) from Brussels. There are two courses, one of 18 holes, one of 9 holes.

Royal Waterloo, Chemin de Wavre About 14 miles (22.5 km) from Brussels. This club, perhaps the most popular in Belgium, moved to this new venue some years ago.

Bolivia

La Paz *See* A–Z, HIGHEST GOLF COURSE IN THE WORLD.

Burma

Rangoon One of the oldest clubs in the Far East, dating from 1905. The course, which measures some 6600 yd (6035 m), is said to be a good test of golf.

Canada

Royal Montreal This is the oldest club in Canada, having been established in 1873. Fittingly it was the venue of the first Canadian Open Championship in 1904. It housed the first Canada Cup match, the forerunner of the World Cup, in 1953.

Royal Quebec This club is one year younger than the Royal Montreal Club, although golf was first played in Canada at Quebec. Curiously it has been favoured with only a few Canadian championships.

Caribbean

Tobago Golf Club, Mount Irvine Bay Hotel, West Indies Opened in March 1969 and is considered the finest course in the East Caribbean. A spacious and open planned clubhouse looks out over the championship course and the coral sands which stretch to Buccoo Reef. A friendly, unspoilt paradise island where the course plays host to major pro-ams.

Ceylon (Sri Lanka)

Royal Colombo This club was established in 1882 due to the influence of British residents on the island in connection with the tea-growing industry. It is one of four clubs in Ceylon. The two championships of the country, the Ladies' and the Amateur, have been shared between Royal Colombo and Nuwara Eliya.

Corfu

Corfu Golf and Country Club Constructed to championship specifications by architect Donald Harradine, it was opened in 1972. A magnificent clubhouse complements the course and offers the golfer all requirements. A great test of golf, with plenty of water around, contributed by a small river and five man-made lakes. A fully automatic watering system ensures that the greens are the finest in the Mediterranean area.

Czechoslovakia

Golf Club Marianské Lázně (Marienbad)   This club, which began in 1904, is important in as much as it is one of the few golf clubs behind the Iron Curtain. Once popular with visitors 'taking the waters', it is now once more flourishing.

Falkland Islands

Stanley Golf Club   This 9-hole course is the most southerly course in the world.

France

Golf de Biarritz   Established in 1888 when Biarritz was a mecca for wealthy British visitors. In recent years it has come back into favour, the French Open Championship having been held there in 1971 and 1972.

Golf de Chantilly, near Paris   An old club, established in 1908. It has housed all the French championships in its time.

Pau   A club which has long passed its centenary, having been formed in 1856. (*See also* HISTORY OF GOLF, p. 16.)

Racing Club de France, Versailles   It was at La Boulie, as this club is popularly known, that the home professional, Arnaud Massy, won the first French Open Championship in 1906. It is still a venue for that event, the 1974 Championship having been played there.

Saint Nom La Breteche, near Paris   A comparatively new club, the course is the work of the British golf-course architect, Fred Hawtree, and it was the venue of the 1963 World Cup.

Holland

Haagsche Golf Club, near The Hague   This club was established in 1893, and is a fine seaside links. The Duch Open Championship has been played at Den Haagsche many times.

Italy

Circolo Golf Olgiata, Olgiata   One of Italy's newest courses, it was opened in 1961, and has already achieved a vast amount of status. The 1968 World Cup was played there and it was the venue of the 1972 Italian Open Championship.

Japan

Kasumigaseki, near Tokyo   Golf was first introduced to Japan by a Scotsman named Groome in 1903, but progress was slow, and the game has only recently started to boom in that country. Kobe was the first club but now perhaps the best known from an international viewpoint is the Kasumigaseki Country Club near Tokyo where the World Cup was held in 1957.

Malaysia

Kuala Lumpur   Kuala Lumpur is not the oldest club in Malaysia—that honour belongs to the Perak Club which goes back to 1888. It is, however, the best-known club and is the venue of the Malaysian Open Championship, an important event in the expanding Far East circuit.

Morocco

Royal Golf Rabat, Dar es-Salaam   Rabat boasts a superb 45-hole complex, with the Red Course being famous for pro-ams and the annual Trophee Hassan II. International architect, Trent Jones, created the layout through the 405-ha cork forest, supported by the enthusiasm of King Hassan II, who is a keen player. The modern luxury clubhouse is certainly fit for a golfing king.

New Zealand

Otago   There has always been a strong Scottish influence in New Zealand and so naturally golf has been played in that country for over a century. The oldest club in the country is Otago which was established in 1871. The Christchurch Club is two years younger.

Portugal

Estoril Many people may well have the idea that Estoril is an old club, but it was in fact founded in 1945. It is especially popular with British visitors. Portugal's other three main courses, Penina and Val do Lobo (Pl. 8), both laid out by Henry Cotton, and Vilamoura are also new courses. The 1973 Portuguese Open Championship was held at the Penina and Vilamoura courses.

South Africa

Royal Cape, Cape Province   Established in 1885. The club became 'Royal' in 1910 and although South Africa is no longer part of the British Commonwealth, the club still keeps the title. It has been the venue of all the South African championships.

Spain

Puerto de Hierro, Madrid   This is one of Madrid's three fine courses and probably the best known. The other two are Real Automobile Club (Pl. 8) and Campo de Golf. Another has recently been constructed. Strangely enough, perhaps because of British influence, the Club de Las Palmas in the Canary Islands dates back as far as 1891.

Switzerland

Crans sur Sierre This is a beautiful course set high in the Alps. The Swiss Open Championship which began in 1923 has been played at Crans since 1939 and attracts an international entry.

Thailand

Royal Bangkok This club must be unique in as much as its first club-house was originally a temple. The club was founded in 1890. Golf has made great strides in Thailand in recent years and some of its professionals have made their marks in international competition.

LIST OF CHAMPIONSHIPS AND OTHER MAJOR EVENTS (With notes)

(Leading British and United States championships are listed here but for detailed information see the A to Z section)

Argentine Amateur Championship   Little is known about golf in Argentina except that it was taken there by British enthusiasts. The first Argentine Championship was played in 1895. Clubs in Argentina include the Jockey Club, Ranelagh, Hurlingham and Smithfield—evidence of the country's British associations. The championship is played annually at different venues. Conditions of entry can vary from year to year. Details can be had from the Argentine Golf Association, Corrientes 538, Piso 110, Buenos Aires, Argentina. It is a match play event.

Argentine Ladies' Championship   An old event dating back to 1904. In its early days it was dominated by British-born golfers. Conditions of entry vary from year to year, as do the venues. Details from Argentine Golf Association. Address as above. It is a match play event.

Argentine Open Championship   An annual 72-hole stroke play event. Conditions of entry, such as to qualifying rounds, can vary. Argentina has produced some famous professionals such as Roberto de Vicenzo who won the British Open Championship in 1967. Information regarding the championship can be had from the Argentine Golf Association, address as above.

Australian Amateur Championship   First played in 1906, and won by the British golfer, the Hon Michael Scott, three times in its first five years. Scott won the British Amateur Championship 27 years later. Former Australian Amateur champions who became noted professionals were Jim Ferrier and Bruce Devlin. The championship is a match play one. Conditions as to qualifying and handicap can vary. There is a different venue each year. Information from Australian Golf Union, P.O. Box 37, Black Rock, Victoria, 3193, Australia.

Australian Ladies' Championship   Instituted 1894. Overseas winners include Miss Veronica Anstey, England (1955), Mrs Marlene Streit, Canada (1963) and Miss Maisie

Mooney, Ireland (1973). It is an annual match play event. Conditions of entry can vary from year to year. These can be obtained from the Australian Ladies' Golf Union, 11 Airedale Avenue, Hawthorn, Victoria, 3122, Australia. The venues are chosen each year.

Australian Open Championship An annual 72-hole stroke play event first played in 1904 when the British amateur, the Hon Michael Scott was the first winner. He won it again in 1907 the same year as he won one of his three Australian Amateur Championships. Conditions as to qualifying tests can vary each year as do the venues. Information from the Australian Golf Union, address as above, or from the Australian Professional Golfers' Association, 102 Alexander Street, Crows Nest, New South Wales, 2065.

Belgian Amateur Championship An annual match play event which originated in 1919. Since 1963 it has been played at the Royal Zoute club. Previously venues had varied. Conditions of entry regarding qualifying tests and handicap limit can vary. Details from the organizers, Belgian Royal Federation of Golf, Chateau de Ravenstein, Tervueren, Brussels.

Belgian Ladies' Championship Held annually at the Royal Zoute club. It is a match play event. Conditions of entry can vary annually. Details from Belgian Royal Federation of Golf as above.

Brazilian Open Championship Played annually at a different venue each year. Many famous players have won the 72-hole stroke play event including Roberto de Vicenzo, Gary Player, Sam Snead, Billy Casper, Bernard Hunt and Peter Alliss. Conditions of entry vary. Information from Brazilian Golf Association, Caixa Postal 2457, São Paulo, and Caixa Postal 2674, Rio de Janeiro, Brazil.

British Amateur Championship   *See* A–Z.

British Boys' Championship   *See* A–Z.

British Girls' Championship   *See* A–Z.

British Ladies' Amateur Championship   *See* A–Z.

British Open Championship   *See* A–Z.

Canadian Amateur Championship An annual event instituted in 1894. Until 1968 it was a match play event. Since then it has taken the form of a 72-hole stroke play event. The venue changes each year as can the conditions of entry. It is organized by the Canadian (Royal) Golf Association, 696 Yonge Street, Toronto, Ontario, Canada.

Canadian Ladies' Championship An annual event dating from 1901. Until 1969 it was a match play event, since when it has been decided by 72 holes stroke play. Venue varies each year, as can conditions of entry relative to handicap limit and handicapping. Information from the Canadian Ladies' Golf Association, 33 River Road, Ottawa, Ontario, Kil 8B9, Canada.

Canadian Open Championship One of the world's leading events. It is stroke play over 72 holes and is held at a different venue each year. Conditions of entry can vary. Information from Canadian Professional Golfers' Association, 696 Yonge Street, Suite 204, Toronto, Ontario, Canada.

Commonwealth Tournament (Ladies) *See* A–Z.

Curtis Cup *See* A–Z.

Dutch Amateur Championship Although the Dutch claim to have originated the game of golf the Dutch Amateur Championship was a late-comer to the championship scene, beginning in 1921. It is an annual match play event. Venues vary each year as can conditions of entry. It is organized by the Dutch Golf Union, 676 van Alkemadelaan, The Hague, Holland.

Dutch Ladies' Championship Founded 1921. It is a match play event. Venues vary as do conditions of entry such as handicap limit. Information from Dutch Golf Union as above. It is played annually.

Dutch Open Championship Instituted in 1912. Venues vary, but not necessarily from year to year. It is a stroke play event over 72 holes although until 1932 it was decided over 36 holes. Information from the Dutch Golf Union as above. Conditions of entry can vary from year to year. It is an annual event.

English Amateur Championship *See* A–Z.

English Open Amateur Stroke Play Championship *See* A–Z.

English Ladies' Championship Instituted in 1912. It is an annual match play event played on a different course each year. It is open to women with English qualifications as laid down by the English Ladies' Golf Association. Such qualifications as well as handicap limit are liable to alteration. There is no qualifying test.

European Amateur Team Championship Inaugurated 1959, this event is played every two years by match play. Venues alternate between the British Isles and the Continent.

French Amateur Championship First played at La Boulie in 1904. It is a match play event, the venues varying from year to year. Conditions of entry can vary from time to time. The championship played annually is organized by French Golf Federation, 11 Rue de Bassano, Paris 16e.

French Ladies' Championship This annual championship which is match play was started in 1909. There is a different venue each year. Conditions of entry which can vary from time to time can be had from the French Golf Federation as above.

French Open Championship The oldest of the Continental Open championships, it was first played at La Boulie in 1906. It is a 72-hole stroke play event, as are all major Open Championships. Conditions of entry can vary, as do the venues. It is played annually. Information can be obtained from the French Golf Federation, address as above.

German Amateur Open Championship This is an open event as distinct from the German National Amateur Championship. Played annually and until 1970 a match play event. Since then it has taken the form of 72 holes stroke play. Conditions of entry, i.e. handicap limit, etc., can vary. Information from German Golf Association, 6202 Wiesbaden-Biebrich, Rheinblickstrasse 24, Germany. The venues vary each year.

German Ladies' Championship This event, which is held annually at different venues, was a match play event until 1970 from its inception in 1936. Then in 1971 it became a 54-hole stroke play event, reverted to match play the following year and in 1973 went back to 54 holes stroke play. Obviously with so many changes in its style, conditions of entry vary. It is organized by the German Golf Association as above.

German Open Championship   Started in 1912 as a 72-hole stroke play event, it is played annually at a different venue. It is organized by the German Golf Association from which body information can be obtained. Address as above. The first winner of the championship in 1912 was the five times British Open Champion, J. H. Taylor. British Professional Percy Alliss won the event four times in succession—1926–9, and three times British Open Champion, Henry Cotton won the title three times in succession, 1937–9.

Indian Amateur Championship   One of the oldest of championships, having originated in 1892. It has always been played at Calcutta Club. It is an annual match play event under conditions laid down by the India Golf Union, Tata Centre (11th floor), 43 Chowringhee Road, Calcutta-16, India, from which body information can be obtained. Conditions of entry vary.

Irish Amateur Championship   *See A–Z.*

Irish Ladies' Championship   An annual match play event which began in 1894. Open to players with Irish qualifications as laid down by the Irish Ladies' Golf Union, 54 Woodlawn Park, Churchtown, Dublin 14. There is no qualifying test but conditions of entry are liable to variation. A different venue each year.

Irish Native Professional Championship   A 72-hole stroke play event, this championship began in 1907. It is played annually at a different venue. Open to Irish professional golfers who fulfil the conditions as drawn up by the Irish Professional Golfers' Association, 36 Kensington Road, Belfast 5. Rules relating to qualifying etc. are liable to variation.

Italian Open Amateur Championship   There are two Italian Amateur Championships, one open to all amateur golfers, the other open only to Italian born amateur golfers. The Open Amateur Championship was instituted in 1906 and its most favoured venue is Villa d'Este. It is held annually and is a match play event under conditions (which change from time to time) laid down by organizers, the Italian Golf Federation, 70 Viale Tiziano, 00100, Rome, Italy. The Italian Native Amateur Championship is also a match play event, played annually under the jurisdiction of the Italian Golf Federation.

Italian Ladies' Championship   With only a few exceptions this championship, which is an annual match play event, has been played at Villa d'Este. Conditions can vary from championship to championship as directed by the Italian Golf Federation, whose address is on p. 166. Information concerning all amateur championships can be obtained from the Federation.

Italian Open Championship   First played in 1925, the championship is a 72-hole annual stroke play event held at a different venue each year. It is organized by the Italian Golf Federation from whom conditions of entry can be obtained.

Japanese Amateur Championship   Although golf has been played in Japan for many years the country is only now enjoying a boom in the game. The Japanese Amateur Championship began in 1930. It is an annual event played on a different course each year. Until 1966 it was a match play event, but since it has been a 72-hole stroke play event. It is run by the Japan Golf Association, 806 Palace Building, Marunouchi, Chiyodaku, Tokyo, Japan.

Japanese Open Championship   This 72-hole stroke play annual championship began in 1927 and has a different venue each year. The championship is run by the Japan Golf Association.

Kenya Amateur Championship   Golf has been played in Kenya for many years, but only now are Kenyan born golfers making an impression. The Kenya Amateur Championship is an annual match play event. The venues vary each year as can the conditions of entry. It is organized by the Kenya Golf Union, P.O. Box 49609, Nairobi, Kenya from which body information concerning it can be obtained.

Kenya Open Championship   This championship is now an important event in the African circuit. The main competitors are British and South African professionals. It is an annual 72-hole stroke play event. Venues vary. The event is organized by the Kenya Golf Union address as above.

Malaysian Open Championship   A 72-hole stroke play event played annually at Kuala Lumpur. Japanese professionals have been the most successful until now. Information and conditions of entry can be had from the Malaysian Golf Association, Royal Selangor Golf Club, Kuala Lumpur.

New Zealand Amateur Championship A very old championship having been first played in 1893. The New Zealand international, Stuart Jones has won it seven times between 1955 and 1971. An annual match play event, it has a different venue each year. The championship is organized by the New Zealand Golf Association, National Bank Buildings, Box 657, Wellington, New Zealand.

New Zealand Ladies' Championship Instituted in 1922, it is an annual match play event with a different venue each year. Information from the New Zealand Ladies' Golf Union, Box 752, Taupo, New Zealand.

New Zealand Open Championship First played in 1907, it is a 72-hole stroke play event, played at a different venue each year. Information from the New Zealand Professional Golfers' Association, Box 33320, Takapuna, Auckland, New Zealand.

Portuguese Open Amateur Championship So called to differentiate from the lesser Portuguese National Amateur championship, this match play event has been played at Estoril every year except in 1967 when it was played at Penina. It is an annual event. The championship is organized by the Portuguese Golf Federation, Estoril Golf Club, Avenida de Republica, Estoril, Portugal.

Portuguese Ladies' Championship Organized by the Portuguese Golf Federation, this annual championship is always played at Estoril. It is a match play event. Conditions of entry can vary from year to year and can be had from the Portuguese Federation, address as above.

Portuguese Open Championship A 72-hole annual stroke play event, it was played at Estoril until 1973 when it was played at Penina. In 1974 it reverted to Estoril. It is controlled by the Portuguese Golf Federation who lay down the conditions of entry which can vary.

Ryder Cup *See A–Z.*

Scandinavian Amateur Championship Instituted in 1956, this championship is an annual match play event played on a different course each year, and in a different country each year, the countries being the three Scandinavian ones, Norway, Sweden and Denmark. Information can be obtained from either the Danish, the Norwegian or the Swedish Golf Unions. Addresses are as follows:

Danish Golf Union—Bella Centret, Hvidkeldevej 64, DK 2400, Copenhagen NV.

Norwegian Golf Union—Post Box 1585, Vika, Oslo, Norway.

Swedish Golf Union—Tysta Gatan 4, 115 24, Stockholm, Sweden.

Scandinavian Enterprises Open Championship Instituted in 1973, it is now an annual event in the professional calendar. It carries substantial prize money and is played over different venues in Scandinavia.

Scandinavian Ladies' Championship An annual match play event played in each of the three Scandinavian countries in turn. Conditions of entry vary. Information from the golf unions as above.

Scottish Amateur Championship *See* A–Z.

Scottish Ladies' Championship Instituted 1903, this is an annual match play event at a different venue each year. It is organized by the Scottish Ladies' Golf Association, Heemstede, Gosford Road, Longniddry, East Lothian. Conditions of entry vary from time to time.

Scottish Professional Championship First played in 1907, this championship is organized by the Scottish Professional Golfers' Association, 78 Fountainhall Road, Aberdeen. It is an annual event played by stroke play over 72 holes. Entry is restricted to professional golfers of Scottish parentage. Venues vary from year to year.

South African Amateur Championship An annual match play event held at a different course each year. Conditions as to handicap limit can vary. Information from the South African Golf Union, P.O. Box 1537, Cape Town.

South African Ladies' Championship While South African men's golf has supplied two of the world's greatest professional golfers in the persons of Bobby Locke and Gary Player, both of whom have scored numerous international successes, South Africa's women golfers have not achieved the same success. The general standard of women's golf in the Union, however, is high. This championship is a match play one and is held annually at a different venue. It is organized by the South African

Ladies' Golf Union, P.O. Box 135, Vereeniging, Transvaal, South Africa. Conditions can vary from year to year.

Spanish Amateur Championship   Organized by the Spanish Golf Association, 9–3 Dcha, Madrid 20, Spain, this is a match play annual event held on a different course each year. It was first played in 1911. Conditions of entry can vary each year.

Spanish Ladies' Championship   Instituted in 1911, it is an annual match play event, the venue of which is chosen each year. Conditions are as laid down each year by the Spanish Golf Association, address as above.

Spanish Open Championship   This championship began in 1912. It is an annual 72-hole stroke play event, the venue of which has previously been chosen each year by the Spanish Golf Federation who can supply information regarding the event. By reason of a contract drawn up with the La Manga Club, the championship will be staged at that club until 1976.

Swiss Amateur Championship   An annual match play event going back to 1907, this championship is staged at a different venue each year. It is organized by the Swiss Golf Association, Postfach, 8035, Zurich, Switzerland. Conditions of entry such as handicap limit can vary from year to year.

Swiss Ladies' Championship   Instituted in 1907, this is an annual match play event played at a different venue each year. It is organized by the Swiss Golf Association address as above.

Swiss Open Championship   This annual 72-hole stroke play championship began in 1923. At first there was a different venue each year but since 1939 it has been played at Crans-sur-Sierre. It is organized by the Swiss Golf Association who decide on the conditions of entry each year.

United States Amateur Championship   *See* A–Z.

United States Ladies' Amateur Championship   *See* A–Z.

United States Ladies' Open Championship   *See* A–Z.

United States Masters Tournament   *See* A–Z (Masters Tournament).

United States Open Championship   *See* A–Z.

United States PGA Championship   *See* A–Z.

Vagliano Trophy Match   A match between the lady golfers of Britain and the lady golfers of Europe. It was inaugurated in 1959 and is played every two years, the venues being alternatively in the British Isles and Europe.

Walker Cup   *See* A–Z.

Welsh Amateur Championship   *See* A–Z.

Welsh Ladies' Championship   A match play event played annually at a different venue each year. It is open to lady golfers of Welsh parentage. Conditions for the championship are laid down by the Welsh Ladies' Golf Union, Ysgoldy Gynt, Llanhennock, Newport, Mon.

Welsh Professional Championship   For professional golfers of Welsh parentage, it is a 72-hole stroke play event organized by the Professional Golfers' Association, (Welsh Section), Pyle and Kenfig Golf Club, Pyle, Glamorganshire. The event is played annually, the venues varying from year to year.

World Cup   *See* A–Z.

World Women's Amateur Team Championship (Also known as the Espirito Trophy)   This competition, in which teams of women golfers from various nations oppose each other, is played every two years in a different country. It was inaugurated in 1964 when France won. Since then United States players have won the competition on every occasion.

CHAMPIONSHIP WINNERS

Also US Masters Winners and Walker Cup and Ryder Cup Results

BRITISH OPEN CHAMPIONSHIP

Number of entries in 1860: 8, in 1973: 569

THE BELT

Year	Winners	Score	Venue
1860	W. Park	174	Prestwick
1861	T. Morris, Sr	163	Prestwick
1862	T. Morris, Sr	163	Prestwick
1863	W. Park	168	Prestwick
1864	T. Morris, Sr	160	Prestwick
1865	A. Strath	162	Prestwick
1866	W. Park	169	Prestwick
1867	T. Morris, Sr	170	Prestwick
1868	T. Morris, Jr	157	Prestwick
1869	T. Morris, Jr	154	Prestwick
1870	T. Morris, Jr	149	Prestwick

THE CUP * Denotes amateur

Year	Winners	Score	Venue
1872	T. Morris, Jr	166	Prestwick
1873	Tom Kidd	179	St Andrews
1874	Mungo Park	159	Musselburgh
1875	Willie Park	166	Prestwick
1876	R. Martin	176	St Andrews
1877	J. Anderson	160	Musselburgh
1878	J. Anderson	157	Prestwick
1879	J. Anderson	170	St Andrews
1880	B. Ferguson	162	Musselburgh
1881	B. Ferguson	170	Prestwick
1882	B. Ferguson	171	St Andrews
1883	W. Fernie	159	Musselburgh
1884	J. Simpson	160	Prestwick
1885	R. Martin	171	St Andrews
1886	D. Brown	157	Musselburgh
1887	W. Park, Jr	161	Prestwick
1888	Jack Burns	171	St Andrews

1889	W. Park	155	Musselburgh
1890	*John Ball	164	Prestwick
1891	Hugh Kirkaldy	166	St Andrews

72 holes played in succeeding years

1892	*H. H. Hilton	305	Muirfield
1893	W. Auchterlonie	322	Prestwick
1894	J. H. Taylor	326	Sandwich
1895	J. H. Taylor	322	St Andrews
1896	H. Vardon	316	Muirfield
1897	*H. H. Hilton	314	Hoylake
1898	H. Vardon	307	Prestwick
1899	H. Vardon	310	Sandwich
1900	J. H. Taylor	309	St Andrews
1901	J. Braid	309	Muirfield
1902	A. Herd	307	Hoylake
1903	H. Vardon	300	Prestwick
1904	J. White	296	Sandwich
1905	J. Braid	318	St Andrews
1906	J. Braid	300	Muirfield
1907	A. Massy	312	Hoylake
1908	J. Braid	291	Prestwick
1909	J. H. Taylor	295	Deal
1910	J. Braid	299	St Andrews
1911	H. Vardon	303	Sandwich
1912	E. Ray	295	Muirfield
1913	J. H. Taylor	304	Hoylake
1914	H. Vardon	306	Prestwick
1915–			
1919	No Championship		
1920	G. Duncan	303	Deal
1921	J. Hutchison	296	St Andrews
1922	W. Hagen	300	Sandwich
1923	A. G. Havers	295	Troon
1924	W. Hagen	301	Hoylake
1925	J. Barnes	300	Prestwick
1926	*R. T. Jones	291	Royal Lytham
1927	*R. T. Jones	285	St Andrews
1928	W. Hagen	292	Sandwich
1929	W. Hagen	292	Muirfield
1930	*R. T. Jones	292	Hoylake
1931	T. D. Armour	296	Carnoustie
1932	G. Sarazen	283	Sandwich
1933	D. Shute	292	St Andrews

1934	T. H. Cotton	283	Sandwich
1935	A. Perry	283	Muirfield
1936	A. H. Padgham	287	Hoylake
1937	T. H. Cotton	290	Carnoustie
1938	R. A. Whitcombe	295	Sandwich
1939	R. Burton	290	St Andrews
1940–			
1945	No Championship		
1946	S. Snead	290	St Andrews
1947	F. Daly	293	Hoylake
1948	T. H. Cotton	284	Muirfield
1949	A. D. Locke	283	Sandwich
1950	A. D. Locke	279	Troon
1951	Max Faulkner	285	Portrush
1952	A. D. Locke	287	Royal Lytham
1953	B. Hogan	282	Carnoustie
1954	Peter Thomson	283	Royal Birkdale
1955	Peter Thomson	281	St Andrews
1956	Peter Thomson	286	Hoylake
1957	A. D. Locke	279	St Andrews
1958	Peter Thomson	278	Royal Lytham
1959	G. J. Player	284	Muirfield
1960	K. D. G. Nagle	278	St Andrews
1961	A. Palmer	284	Royal Birkdale
1962	A. Palmer	276	Troon
1963	Bob Charles	277	Royal Lytham
1964	T. Lema	279	St Andrews
1965	Peter Thomson	285	Royal Birkdale
1966	J. Nicklaus	282	Muirfield
1967	R. de Vicenzo	278	Hoylake
1968	G. J. Player	289	Carnoustie
1969	A. Jacklin	280	Royal Lytham
1970	J. Nicklaus	283	St Andrews
1971	Lee Trevino	278	Royal Birkdale
1972	Lee Trevino	278	Muirfield
1973	T. Weiskopf	276	Troon
1974	G. J. Player	282	Royal Lytham
1975	T. Watson	279	Carnoustie
1976	J. Miller	279	Royal Birkdale
1977			
1978			

BRITISH AMATEUR CHAMPIONSHIP

Year	Winners	Venue
1885	A. F. Macfie	Hoylake
1886	H. G. Hutchinson	St Andrews
1887	H. G. Hutchinson	Hoylake
1888	John Ball	Prestwick
1889	J. E. Laidlay	St Andrews
1890	John Ball	Hoylake
1891	J. E. Laidlay	St Andrews
1892	John Ball	Sandwich
1893	Peter Anderson	Prestwick
1894	John Ball	Hoylake
1895	L. M. B. Melville	St Andrews

In the following years Final extended to 36 holes

Year	Winners	Venue
1896	F. G. Tait	Sandwich
1897	A. J. T. Allan	Muirfield
1898	F. G. Tait	Hoylake
1899	John Ball	Prestwick
1900	H. H. Hilton	Sandwich
1901	H. H. Hilton	St Andrews
1902	C. Hutchings	Hoylake
1903	R. Maxwell	Muirfield
1904	W. J. Travis	Sandwich
1905	A. G. Barry	Prestwick
1906	James Robb	Hoylake
1907	John Ball	St Andrews
1908	E. A. Lassen	Sandwich
1909	R. Maxwell	Muirfield
1910	John Ball	Hoylake
1911	H. H. Hilton	Prestwick
1912	John Ball	Westward Ho!
1913	H. H. Hilton	St Andrews
1914	J. L. C. Jenkins	Sandwich
1915–		
1919	No Championship	
1920	C. J. H. Tolley	Muirfield
1921	W. I. Hunter	Hoylake
1922	E. W. E. Holderness	Prestwick
1923	R. H. Wethered	Deal
1924	E. W. E. Holderness	St Andrews
1925	Robert Harris	Westward Ho!
1926	Jesse Sweetser	Muirfield
1927	Dr W. Tweddell	Hoylake
1928	T. P. Perkins	Prestwick
1929	C. J. H. Tolley	Sandwich

1930	R. T. Jones	St Andrews
1931	E. Martin Smith	Westward Ho!
1932	John de Forest	Muirfield
1933	Hon. M. Scott	Hoylake
1934	W. Lawson Little	Prestwick
1935	W. Lawson Little	Royal Lytham
1936	H. Thomson	St Andrews
1937	R. Sweeney, Jr	Sandwich
1938	C. R. Yates	Troon
1939	A. T. Kyle	Hoylake
1940–		
1945	No Championship	
1946	Jas. Bruen	Birkdale
1947	W. Turnesa	Carnoustie
1948	F. Stranahan	Sandwich
1949	S. M. McCready	Portmarnock
1950	F. Stranahan	St Andrews
1951	R. D. Chapman	Porthcawl
1952	E. Harvie Ward	Prestwick
1953	J. B. Carr	Hoylake
1954	D. Bachli	Muirfield
1955	Jos. W. Conrad	Royal Lytham
1956	J. Beharrell	Troon
1957	R. Reid Jack	Formby
1958	J. B. Carr	St Andrews
1959	D. R. Beman	Sandwich
1960	J. B. Carr	Portrush
1961	M. F. Bonallack	Turnberry
1962	R. D. Davies	Hoylake
1963	M. S. R. Lunt	St Andrews
1964	Gordon J. Clark	Ganton
1965	M. F. Bonallack	Porthcawl
1966	R. E. Cole	Carnoustie
1967	R. B. Dickson	Formby
1968	M. F. Bonallack	Troon
1969	M. F. Bonallack	Hoylake
1970	M. F. Bonallack	Newcastle, Co. Down
1971	S. Melnyk	Carnoustie
1972	Trevor Homer	Sandwich
1973	R. Siderowf	Royal Porthcawl
1974	Trevor Homer	Muirfield
1975	M. Giles	Hoylake
1976	R. Siderowf	St Andrews
1977		
1978		

BRITISH LADIES' AMATEUR CHAMPIONSHIP

Year	Winners	Venue
1893	Lady Margaret Scott	St Annes
1894	Lady Margaret Scott	Littlestone
1895	Lady Margaret Scott	Portrush
1896	Miss Pascoe	Hoylake
1897	Miss E. C. Orr	Gullane
1898	Miss L. Thomson	Yarmouth
1899	Miss M. Hezlet	Newcastle, Co. Down
1900	Miss Adair	Westward Ho!
1901	Miss Graham	Aberdovey
1902	Miss M. Hezlet	Deal
1903	Miss Adair	Portrush
1904	Miss L. Dod	Troon
1905	Miss B. Thompson	Cromer
1906	Mrs Kennion	Burnham
1907	Miss M. Hezlet	Newcastle, Co. Down
1908	Miss M. Titterton	St Andrews
1909	Miss D. Campbell	Royal Birkdale
1910	Miss Grant Suttie	Westward Ho!
1911	Miss D. Campbell	Portrush
1912	Miss G. Ravenscroft	Turnberry
1913	Miss M. Dodd	Royal Lytham
1914	Miss C. Leitch	Hunstanton
1915–		
1919	No Championship	
1920	Miss C. Leitch	Newcastle, Co. Down
1921	Miss C. Leitch	Turnberry
1922	Miss J. Wethered	Princes, Sandwich
1923	Miss D. Chambers	Burnham
1924	Miss J. Wethered	Portrush
1925	Miss J. Wethered	Troon
1926	Miss C. Leitch	Harlech
1927	Mlle Thion de la Chaume	Newcastle, Co. Down
1928	Mlle Nanette Le Blan	Hunstanton
1929	Miss J. Wethered	St Andrews
1930	Miss D. Fishwick	Formby
1931	Miss E. Wilson	Portmarnock
1932	Miss E. Wilson	Saunton
1933	Miss E. Wilson	Gleneagles
1934	Mrs A. M. Holm	Royal Porthcawl
1935	Miss W. Morgan	Newcastle, Co. Down
1936	Miss P. Barton	Portrush
1937	Miss J. Anderson	Turnberry
1938	Mrs A. M. Holm	Burnham
1939	Miss P. Barton	Portrush

1940–		
1945	No Championship	
1946	Mrs G. W. Hetherington	Hunstanton
1947	Mrs George Zaharias	Gullane
1948	Miss Louise Suggs	Royal Lytham
1949	Miss Frances Stephens	Harlech
1950	Vicomtesse de Saint Sauveur	Newcastle, Co. Down
1951	Mrs P. G. MacCann	Broadstone
1952	Miss M. Paterson	Troon
1953	Miss M. Stewart	Royal Porthcawl
1954	Miss F. Stephens	Ganton
1955	Mrs G. Valentine	Royal Portrush
1956	Miss M. Smith	Sunningdale
1957	Miss P. Garvey	Gleneagles
1958	Mrs G. Valentine	Hunstanton
1959	Miss E. Price	Berkshire
1960	Miss B. McIntire	Harlech
1961	Mrs A. D. Spearman	Carnoustie
1962	Mrs A. D. Spearman	Royal Birkdale
1963	Mlle B. Varangot	Newcastle, Co Down
1964	Miss C. Sorensen	Princes, Sandwich
1965	Mlle B. Varangot	St Andrews
1966	Miss E. Chadwick	Ganton
1967	Miss E. Chadwick	Harlech
1968	Mlle B. Varangot	Walton Heath
1969	Mlle C. Lacoste	Royal Portrush
1970	Miss D. Oxley	Gullane
1971	Miss Michelle Walker	Alwoodley
1972	Miss Michelle Walker	Hunstanton
1973	Miss A. Irvin	Carnoustie
1974	Miss C. Semple	Royal Porthcawl
1975	Miss Nancy Roth Syms	St Andrews
1976	Miss C. Panton	Silloth
1977		
1978		

UNITED STATES OPEN CHAMPIONSHIP

*Denotes amateur

Year	Winners	Score	Venue
1895	Horace Rawlins	173	Newport G.C., Newport, R.I.
1896	James Foulis	152	Shinnecock Hills G.C., Southampton, N.Y.
1897	Joe Lloyd	162	Chicago G.C., Wheaton, Ill.
1898	Fred Herd	328	Myopia Hunt C., S. Hamilton, Mass.
1899	Willie Smith	315	Baltimore, C.C., Baltimore, Md.
1900	Harry Vardon	313	Chicago G.C., Wheaton, Ill.
1901	Willie Anderson	331	Myopia Hunt C., S. Hamilton, Mass.
1902	Lawrence Auchterlonie	307	Garden City G.C., Garden City, N.Y.
1903	Willie Anderson	307	Baltusrol G.C., Springfield, N.J.
1904	Willie Anderson	303	Glen View C., Golf, Ill.
1905	Willie Anderson	314	Myopia Hunt C., S. Hamilton, Mass.
1906	Alex Smith	295	Onwentsia C., Lake Forest, Ill.
1907	Alex Ross	302	Philadelphia Cricket C., Philadelphia, Pa.
1908	Fred McLeod	322	Myopia Hunt C., S. Hamilton, Mass.
1909	George Sargent	290	Englewood G.C., Englewood, N.J.
1910	Alex Smith	298	Philadelphia Cricket C., St Martins, Pa.
1911	John J. McDermott	307	Chicago G.C., Wheaton, Ill.
1912	John J. McDermott	294	C.C. of Buffalo, Buffalo, N.Y.
1913	*Francis Ouimet	304	The Country Club, Brookline, Mass.
1914	Walter Hagen	290	Midlothian C.C., Blue Island, Ill.
1915	*Jerome D. Travers	297	Baltusrol G.C., Springfield, N.J.
1916	*Charles Evans, Jr	286	Minikahda Club, Minneapolis, Minn.
1917–			
1918	No Championship		
1919	Walter Hagen	301	Brae Burn C.C., West Newton, Mass.

1920	Edward Ray	295	Inverness Club, Toledo, Ohio
1921	James M. Barnes	289	Columbia C.C., Chevy Chase, Md.
1922	Gene Sarazen	288	Skokie C.C., Glencoe, Ill.
1923	*Robert T. Jones, Jr	296	Inwood C.C., Inwood, N.Y.
1924	Cyril Walker	297	Oakland Hills C.C., Birmingham, Mich.
1925	William Macfarlane	291	Worcester C.C., Worcester, Mass.
1926	*Robert T. Jones, Jr	293	Scioto C.C., Columbus, Ohio
1927	Tommy Armour	301	Oakmont C.C., Oakmont, Pa.
1928	Johnny Farrell	294	Olympia Fields C.C., Mateson, Ill.
1929	*Robert T. Jones, Jr	294	Winged Foot G.C., Mamaroneck, N.Y.
1930	*Robert T. Jones, Jr	287	Interlachen C.C., Minneapolis, Minn.
1931	Billy Burke	292	Inverness Club, Toledo, Ohio
1932	Gene Sarazen	286	Fresh Meadow C.C., Flushing, N.Y.
1933	*John G. Goodman	287	North Shore G.C., Glen View, Ill.
1934	Olin Dutra	293	Merion Cricket C., Ardmore, Pa.
1935	Sam Parks, Jr	299	Oakmont C.C., Oakmont, Pa.
1936	Tony Manero	282	Baltusrol G.C. (Lower Course), Springfield, N.Y.
1937	Ralph Guldahl	281	Oakland Hills C.C., Birmingham, Mich.
1938	Ralph Guldahl	284	Cherry Hills Club, Denver, Colo.
1939	Byron Nelson	284	Philadelphia Country C., West Conshohocken, Pa.
1940	Lawson Little	287	Canterbury G.C., Cleveland, Ohio
1941	Craig Wood	284	Colonial Club, Fort Worth, Texas
1942– 1945	No Championship		
1946	Lloyd Mangrum	284	Canterbury G.C., Cleveland, Ohio
1947	Lew Worsham	282	St Louis C.C., Clayton, Mo.
1948	Ben Hogan	276	Riviera C.C., Los Angeles, Calif.
1949	Cary Middlecoff	286	Medinah C.C., Medinah, Ill.
1950	Ben Hogan	287	Merion G.C., Ardmore, Pa.

1951	Ben Hogan	287	Oakland Hills C.C., Birmingham, Mich.
1952	Julius Boros	281	Northwood C., Dallas, Texas
1953	Ben Hogan	283	Oakmont C.C., Oakmont, Pa.
1954	Ed Furgol	284	Baltusrol G.C. (Lower Course), Springfield, N.J.
1955	Jack Fleck	287	Olympic C.C., San Francisco, Calif.
1956	Cary Middlecoff	281	Oak Hill C.C. (East Course),
1957	Dick Mayer	282	Inverness Club, Toledo, Ohio
1958	Tommy Bolt	283	Southern Hills C.C., Tulsa, Okla.
1959	Bill Casper, Jr	282	Winged Foot G.C., Mamaroneck, N.Y.
1960	Arnold Palmer	280	Cherry Hills C.C., Englewood, Colo.
1961	Gene Littler	281	Oakland Hills C.C., Birmingham, Mich.
1962	Jack Nicklaus	283	Oakmont C.C., Oakmont, Pa.
1963	Julius Boros	293	The Country Club, Brookline, Mass.
1964	Ken Venturi	278	Congressional C.C., Washington, D.C.
1965	Gary Player	282	Bellerive C.C., St Louis, Mo.
1966	Bill Casper, Jr	278	Olympic C.C., San Francisco, Calif.
1967	Jack Nicklaus	275	Baltusrol G.C. (Lower Course), Springfield, N.J.
1968	Lee Trevino	275	Oak Hill C.C. (East Course), Rochester, N.Y.
1969	Orville Moody	281	Champions G.C., Houston, Texas
1970	Tony Jacklin	281	Hazeltine National G.C., Chaska, Minn.
1971	Lee Trevino	280	Merion G.C. (East Course), Ardmore, Pa.
1972	Jack Nicklaus	290	Pebble Beach, California
1973	Johnny Miller	279	Oakmont, P.A.
1974	Hale Irwin	287	Winged Foot, N.Y.
1975	L. Graham		Medinah C.C.
1976	J. Pate	277	Atlanta Athletic C.C. Ga.
1977			
1978			

UNITED STATES AMATEUR CHAMPIONSHIP

Year	Winners	Venue
1895	Charles B. Macdonald	Newport G.C., Newport, R.I. All Match Play
1896	H. J. Whigham	Shinnecock Hills G.C., Southampton, N.Y.
1897	H. J. Whigham	Chicago G.C., Wheaton, Ill.
1898	Findlay S. Douglas	Morris County G.C., Morristown, N.J.
1899	H. M. Harriman	Onwentsia Club, Lake Forest, Ill.
1900	Walter J. Travis	Garden City G.C., Garden City, N.Y.
1901	Walter J. Travis	C.C. of Atlantic City, Atlantic City, N.J.
1902	Louis N. James	Glen View Club, Golf, Ill.
1903	Walter J. Travis	Nassau C.C., Glen Cove, N.Y. All Match Play
1904	H. Chandler Egan	Baltusrol G.C., Springfield, N.J.
1905	H. Chandler Egan	Chicago G.C., Wheaton, Ill.
1906	Eben M. Byers	Englewood G.C., Englewood, N.J.
1907	Jerome D. Travers	Euclid Club, Cleveland, Ohio
1908	Jerome D. Travers	Garden City G.C., Garden City, N.Y.
1909	Robert A. Gardner	Chicago G.C., Wheaton, Ill.
1910	William C. Fownes, Jr	The Country Club, Brookline, Mass.
1911	Harold H. Hilton	The Apawamis Club, Rye, N.Y.
1912	Jerome D. Travers	Chicago G.C., Wheaton, Ill.
1913	Jerome D. Travers	Garden City G.C., Garden City, N.Y.
1914	Francis Ouimet	Ekwanok C.C., Manchester, Vt.
1915	Robert A. Gardner	C.C. of Detroit, Grosse Pointe Farms, Mich.
1916	Charles Evans, Jr	Merion Cricket C., Haverford, Pa.
1917– 1918	No Championship	
1919	S. Davidson Herron	Oakmont C.C., Pittsburgh, Pa.
1920	Charles Evans, Jr	Engineers' C.C., Roslyn, N.Y.
1921	Jesse P. Guilford	St Louis C.C., Clayton, Mo.
1922	Jess W. Sweetser	The Country Club, Brookline, Mass.
1923	Max R. Marston	Flossmoor C.C., Flossmoor, Ill.
1924	Robert T. Jones, Jr	Merion Cricket C., Ardmore, Pa.
1925	Robert T. Jones, Jr	Oakmont C.C., Oakmont, Pa.
1926	George Von Elm	Baltusrol G.C., Springfield, N.J.
1927	Robert T. Jones, Jr	Minikahda Club, Minneapolis, Minn.
1928	Robert T. Jones, Jr	Brae Burn C.C., West Newton, Mass.
1929	Harrison R. Johnston	Del Monte Golf and C.C., Pebble Beach, Calif.

1930	Robert T. Jones, Jr	Merion Cricket C., Ardmore, Pa.
1931	Francis Ouimet	Beverly C.C., Chicago, Ill.
1932	C. Ross Somerville	Baltimore C.C., Five Farms Course, Md.
1933	George T. Dunlap, Jr	Kenwood C.C., Cincinnati, Ohio
1934	W. Lawson Little, Jr	The Country Club, Brookline, Mass. All Match Play
1935	W. Lawson Little, Jr	The Country Club, Cleveland, Ohio All Match Play
1936	John W. Fischer	Garden City G.C., Garden City, N.Y. All Match Play
1937	John Goodman	Alderwood C.C., Portland, Ore.
1938	William P. Turnesa	Oakmont C.C., Oakmont, Pa.
1939	Marvin H. Ward	North Shore C.C., Glen View, Ill.
1940	Richard D. Chapman	Winged Foot, N.Y. Mamaroneck, N.Y.
1941	Marvin H. Ward	Omaha Field C., Omaha, Neb.
1942–1945	No Championship	
1946	Stanley E. (Ted) Bishop	Baltusrol G.C., Springfield, N.J.

All Match Play 1947–1963

1947	Robert H. (Skee) Riegel	Del Monte G. and C.C., Pebble Beach, Calif.
1948	William P. Turnesa	Memphis C.C., Memphis, Tenn.
1949	Charles R. Coe	Oak Hill C.C., Rochester, N.Y.
1950	Sam Urzetta	Minneapolis G.C., Minneapolis, Minn.
1951	Billy Maxwell	Saucon Valley C.C., Bethlehem, Pa.
1952	Jack Westland	Seattle G.C., Seattle, Wash.
1953	Gene A. Littler	Oklahoma City G. and C.C., Oklahoma City, Okla.
1954	Arnold D. Palmer	C.C. of Detroit, Grosse Pointe Farms, Mich.
1955	E. Harvie Ward, Jr	C.C. of Virginia, Richmond, Va.
1956	E. Harvie Ward, Jr	Knollwood C., Lake Forest, Ill.
1957	Hillman Robbins, Jr	The Country Club, Brookline, Mass.
1958	Charles R. Coe	Olympic C.C., San Francisco, Calif.
1959	Jack W. Nicklaus	Broadmoor G.C. (East Course), Colorado Springs, Colo.
1960	Deane R. Beman	St Louis C.C., Clayton, Mo.
1961	Jack W. Nicklaus	Pebble Beach G.L., Pebble Beach, Calif.
1962	Labron E. Harris, Jr	Pinehurst C.C. (No. 2 Course), Pinehurst, N.C.
1963	Deane R. Beman	Wakonda Club, Des Moines, Iowa
1964	William C. Campbell	Canterbury G.C., Cleveland, Ohio

All Stroke Play

1965	Robert J. Murphy, Jr	291	Southern Hills C.C., Tulsa, Okla.
1966	Gary Cowan	285	Merion G.C., Ardmore, Pa.
1967	Robert B. Dickson	285	Broadmoor G.C. (West Course), Colorado Springs, Colo.
1968	Bruce Fleisher	284	Scioto C.C., Columbus, Ohio
1969	Steven N. Melnyk	286	Oakmont C.C., Oakmont, Pa.
1970	Lanny Wadkins	279	Waverley C.C., Portland, Ore.
1971	Gary Cowan	280	Wilmington C.C. (South Course), Wilmington, Del.
1972	Marvin Giles, III	283	Charlotte C.C., Charlotte, N.C.

Reverted to Match Play

1973	C. Stadler	Charlotte, N.C.
1974	J. Pate	Ridgewood, N.J.
1975	F. Ridley	Richmond, Va.
1976	B. Sander	Bel Air G.C., Los Angeles, Calif.
1977		
1978		

UNITED STATES WOMEN'S AMATEUR CHAMPIONSHIP

Year	Winners	Score	Venue
1895	Mrs C. S. Brown	132	Meadow Brook Club, Hempstead, N.Y. Championship, 18 holes, stroke play.

Match Play			Venue
1896	Miss Beatrix Hoyt		Morris County G.C., Morristown, N.J.
1897	Miss Beatrix Hoyt		Essex County Club, Manchester, Mass.
1898	Miss Beatrix Hoyt		Ardsley Club, Ardsley-on-Hudson, N.Y.
1899	Miss Ruth Underhill		Philadelphia Country C., Philadelphia, Pa.
1900	Miss Frances C. Griscom		Shinnecock Hills G.C., Shinnecock Hills, N.Y.
1901	Miss Genevieve Hecker		Baltusrol G.C., Springfield, N.J.
1902	Miss Genevieve Hecker		The Country Club, Brookline, Mass.
1903	Miss Bessie Anthony		Chicago G.C., Wheaton, Ill.
1904	Miss Georgianna M. Bishop		Merion Cricket C., Haverford, Pa.
1905	Miss Pauline Mackay		Morris County G.C., Convent, N.J.
1906	Miss Harriet S. Curtis		Brae Burn C.C., West Newton, Mass.
1907	Miss Margaret Curtis		Midlothian C.C., Blue Island, Ill.
1908	Miss Katherine C. Harley		Chevy Chase Club, Chevy Chase, Md.
1909	Miss Dorothy I. Campbell		Merion Cricket C., Haverford, Pa.
1910	Miss Dorothy I. Campbell		Homewood C.C., Flossmoor, Ill.
1911	Miss Margaret Curtis		Baltusrol G.C., Springfield, N.J.
1912	Miss Margaret Curtis		Essex County Club, Manchester, Mass.
1913	Miss Gladys Ravenscroft		Wilmington C.C., Wilmington, Del.
1914	Mrs H. Arnold Jackson		Nassau C.C., Glen Cove, N.Y.
1915	Mrs C. H. Vanderbeck		Onwentsia Club, Lake Forest, Ill.
1916	Miss Alexa Stirling		Belmont Springs C.C., Waverley, Mass.
1917– 1918	No Championship		
1919	Miss Alexa Stirling		Shawnee C.C., Shawnee-on-Delaware, Pa.
1920	Miss Alexa Stirling		Mayfield C.C., Cleveland, Ohio

1921	Miss Marion Hollins	Hollywood G.C., Deal, N.J.
1922	Miss Glenna Collett	Greenbrier G.C., White Sulphur Springs, W. Va.
1923	Miss Edith Cummings	Westchester-Biltmore C.C., Rye, N.Y.
1924	Mrs Dorothy C. Hurd	Rhode Island C.C., Nyatt, R.I.
1925	Miss Glenna Collett	St Louis C.C., Clayton, Mo.
1926	Mrs G. Henry Stetson	Merion Cricket C., Ardmore, Pa.
1927	Mrs Miriam Burns Horn	Cherry Valley Club, Garden City, N.Y.
1928	Miss Glenna Collett	Va Hot Springs G. and T.C., Hot Springs, Va.
1929	Miss Glenna Collett	Oakland Hills C.C., Birmingham, Mich.
1930	Miss Glenna Collett	Los Angeles C.C., Beverley Hills, Calif.
1931	Miss Helen Hicks	C.C. of Buffalo, Williamsville, N.Y.
1932	Miss Virginia Van Wie	Salem C.C., Peabody, Mass.
1933	Miss Virginia Van Wie	Exmoor C.C., Highland Park, Ill.
1934	Miss Virginia Van Wie	Whitemarsh Valley C.C., Chestnut Hill, Pa.
1935	Mrs Edwin H. Vare, Jr	Interlachen C.C., Hopkins, Minn.
1936	Miss Pamela Barton	Canoe Brook C.C., Summit, N.J.
1937	Mrs Julius A. Page, Jr	Memphis C.C., Memphis, Tenn.
1938	Miss Patty Berg	Westmoreland C.C., Wilmette, Ill.
1939	Miss Betty Jameson	Wee Burn Club, Darien, Conn.
1940	Miss Betty Jameson	Del Monte G. and C.C., Pebble Beach, Calif.
1941	Mrs Frank Newell	The Country Club, Brookline, Mass.
1942– 1945	No Championship	
1946	Mrs George Zaharias	Southern Hills C.C., Tulsa, Okla.
1947	Miss Louise Suggs	Franklin Hills C.C., Franklin, Mich.
1948	Miss Grace S. Lenczyk	Del Monte G. and C.C., Del Monte, Calif.
1949	Mrs Mark A. Porter	Merion G.C., Ardmore, Pa.
1950	Miss Beverly Hanson	Atlanta A.C. (East Lake), Atlanta, Ga.
1951	Miss Dorothy Kirby	Town and C.C., St Paul, Minn.
1952	Mrs Jacqueline Pung	Waverley C.C., Portland, Ore.

All Match Play 1953–63

1953	Miss Mary Lena Faulk	Rhode Island C.C., West Barrington, R.I.
1954	Miss Barbara Romack	Allegheny C.C., Sewickley, Pa.
1955	Miss Patricia A. Lesser	Myers Park C.C., Charlotte, N.C.,

1956	Miss Marlene Stewart	Meridian Hills C.C., Indianapolis, Ind.
1957	Miss Jo Anne Gunderson	Del Paso C.C., Sacramento, Calif.
1958	Miss Anne Quast	Wee Burn C.C., Darien, Conn.
1959	Miss Barbara McIntire	Congressional C.C., Washington, D.C.
1960	Miss Jo Anne Gunderson	Tulsa C.C., Tulsa, Okla.
1961	Mrs Jay D. Decker	Tacoma C. and G.C., Tacoma, Wash.
1962	Miss Jo Anne Gunderson	C.C. of Rochester, Rochester, N.Y.
1963	Mrs David Welts	Taconic Golf Club, Williamstown, Mass.
1964	Miss Barbara McIntire	Prairie Dunes C.C., Hutchinson, Kans.
1965	Miss Jean Ashley	Lakewood C.C., Denver, Colo.
1966	Mrs Jo Anne Carner	Sewickley Heights G.C., Sewickley, Pa.
1967	Miss Mary Lou Dill	Annandale G.C., Pasadena, Calif.
1968	Mrs Jo Anne Carner	Birmingham C.C., Birmingham, Mich.
1969	Miss Catherine Lacoste	Las Colinas C.C., Irving, Texas
1970	Miss Martha Wilkinson	Wee Burn C.C., Darien, Conn.
1971	Miss Laura Baugh	Atlanta C.C., Atlanta, Ga.
1972	Miss M. Budke	St Louis, Missouri
1973	Miss C. Semple	Montclair, N.J.
1974	Miss C. Hill	Broadmoor, Seattle
1975	Miss B. Daniel	Brae Burn, West Newton, Mass.
1976	Miss D. Horton	Del Paso G.C., Sacramento, Calif.
1977		
1978		

THE MASTERS

Venue   Always played at Augusta National Course

Year	Winners	Score
1934	Horton Smith	284
1935	Gene Sarazen	282
1936	Horton Smith	285
1937	Byron Nelson	283
1938	Henry Picard	285
1939	Ralph Guldahl	279
1940	Jimmy Demaret	280
1941	Craig Wood	280
1942	Byron Nelson	280
1943–1945	No Tournaments	
1946	Herman Keiser	282
1947	Jimmy Demaret	281
1948	Claude Harmon	279
1949	Sam Snead	283
1950	Jimmy Demaret	282
1951	Ben Hogan	280
1952	Sam Snead	286
1953	Ben Hogan	274
1954	Sam Snead	289
1955	Cary Middlecoff	279
1956	Jack Burke, Jr	289
1957	Doug Ford	283
1958	Arnold Palmer	284
1959	Art Wall	284
1960	Arnold Palmer	282
1961	Gary Player	280
1962	Arnold Palmer	280
1963	Jack Nicklaus	286
1964	Arnold Palmer	276
1965	Jack Nicklaus	271
1966	Jack Nicklaus	288
1967	Gay Brewer	280
1968	Bob Goalby	277
1969	George Archer	281
1970	Billy Casper	279
1971	Charles Coody	279
1972	Jack Nicklaus	286
1973	Tommy Aaron	283
1974	Gary Player	278
1975	Jack Nicklaus	276
1976	Ray Floyd	271
1977		
1978		

UNITED STATES P.G.A. CHAMPIONSHIP

Year	Winners	Venue
1916	James M. Barnes	Siwanoy C.C., Bronxville, N.Y.
1917–		
1918	No Championship	
1919	James M. Barnes	Engineers C.C., Roslyn, L.I., N.Y.
1920	Jock Hutchison	Flossmoor C.C., Flossmore, Ill.
1921	Walter Hagen	Inwood C.C., Far Rockaway, N.Y.
1922	Gene Sarazen	Oakmont C.C., Oakmont, Pa.
1923	Gene Sarazen	Pelham C.C., Pelham, N.Y.
1924	Walter Hagen	French Lick C.C., French Lick, Ind.
1925	Walter Hagen	Olympia Fields, Olympia Fields, Ill.
1926	Walter Hagen	Salisbury G.C., Westbury, L.I., N.Y.
1927	Walter Hagen	Cedar Crest C.C., Dallas, Texas
1928	Leo Diegel	Five Farms C.C., Baltimore, Md.
1929	Leo Diegel	Hillcrest C.C., Los Angeles, Calif.
1930	Tommy Armour	Fresh Meadows C.C., Flushing, N.Y.
1931	Tom Creavy	Wannamoisett C.C., Rumford, R.I.
1932	Olin Dutra	Keller G.C., St Paul, Minn.
1933	Gene Sarazen	Blue Mound C.C., Milwaukee, Wis.
1934	Paul Runyan	Park C.C., Williamsville, N.Y.
1935	Johnny Revolta	Twin Hills C.C., Oklahoma City, Okla.
1936	Denny Shute	Pinehurst C.C., Pinehurst, N.C.
1937	Denny Shute	Pittsburgh F.C., Aspinwall, Pa.
1938	Paul Runyan	Shawnee C.C., Shawnee-on-Delaware, Pa.
1939	Henry Picard	Pomonok C.C., Flushing, L.I., N.Y.
1940	Byron Nelson	Hershey C.C., Hershey, Pa.
1941	Vic Ghezzi	Cherry Hills C.C., Denver, Colo.
1942	Sam Snead	Seaview C.C., Atlantic City, N.J.
1943	No Championship	
1944	Bob Hamilton	Manito G. and C.C., Spokane, Wash.
1945	Byron Nelson	Morraine C.C., Dayton, Ohio
1946	Ben Hogan	Portland G.C., Portland, Ore.
1947	Jim Ferrier	Plum Hollow C.C., Detroit, Mich.
1948	Ben Hogan	Norwood Hills C.C., St Louis, Mo.
1949	Sam Snead	Hermitage C.C., Richmond, Va.
1950	Chandler Harper	Sciota C.C., Columbus, Ohio
1951	Sam Snead	Oakmont C.C., Oakmont, Pa.
1952	Jim Turnesa	Big Spring C.C., Louisville, Ky.
1953	Walter Burkemo	Birmingham C.C., Birmingham, Mich.
1954	Chick Harbert	Keller G.C., St Paul, Minn.

1955	Doug Ford		Meadowbrook C.C., Detroit, Mich.
1956	Jack Burke		Blue Hill C.C., Boston, Mass.
1957	Lionel Hebert		Miami Valley C.C., Dayton, Ohio

All Stroke Play

1958	Dow Finsterwald	276	Llanerch C.C., Havertown, Pa.
1959	Bob Rosburg	277	Minneapolis G.C., St Louis Park. Minn.
1960	Jay Hebert	281	Firestone C.C., Akron, Ohio
1961	Jerry Barber	277	Olympia Fields C.C., Olympia Fields, Ill.
1962	Gary Player	278	Aronomink G.C., Newtown Square, Pa.
1963	Jack Nicklaus	279	Dallas Athletic Club C.C., Dallas, Tex.
1964	Bobby Nichols	271	Columbus C.C., Columbus, Ohio
1965	Dave Marr	280	Laurel Valley C.C., Ligonier, Pa.
1966	Al Geiberger	280	Firestone G. and C.C., Akron, Ohio
1967	Don January	281	Columbine C.C., Littleton, Colo.
1968	Julius Boros	281	Pecan Valley C.C., San Antonio, Tex.
1969	Ray Floyd	276	N.C.R.C.C., Dayton, Ohio
1970	Dave Stockton	279	Southern Hills C.C., Tulsa, Okla.
1971	Jack Nicklaus	281	P.G.A. National G.C., Palm Beach Gardens, Fla.
1972	Gary Player	281	Birmingham, Michigan
1973	Jack Nicklaus	277	Cleveland, Ohio
1974	Lee Trevino	276	Tanglewood, N.C.
1975	Jack Nicklaus	276	Akron, Ohio
1976	Dave Stockton	281	Congressional C.C., Washington, DC.
1977			
1978			

WALKER CUP MATCH

Year	Score	Venue
1922	U.S., 8; G.B., 4	National Golf Links of America, Southampton, N.Y.
1923	U.S., 6; G.B., 5 one match halved	St Andrews, Scotland
1924	U.S., 9; G.B., 3	Garden City Golf Club, Garden City, N.Y.

1926	U.S., 6; G.B., 5 one match halved	St Andrews, Scotland
1928	U.S., 11; G.B., 1	Chicago Golf Club, Wheaton, Ill.
1930	U.S., 10; G.B., 2	Royal St George's G.C., Sandwich
1932	U.S., 8; G.B., 1	The Country Club, Brookline, Mass.
1934	U.S., 9; G.B., 2 one match halved	St Andrews, Scotland
1936	U.S., 9; G.B., 0 three matches halved	Pine Valley Golf Club, Clementon, N.J.
1938	G.B., 7; U.S., 4 one match halved	St Andrews, Scotland
1940– 1946	No matches	
1947	U.S., 8; G.B., 4	St Andrews, Scotland
1949	U.S., 10; G.B., 2	Winged Foot G.C., Mamaroneck, N.Y.
1951	U.S., 6; G.B., 3 three matches halved	Royal Birkdale
1953	U.S., 9; G.B., 3	Kittansett, Marion, Mass.
1955	U.S., 10; G.B., 2	St Andrews, Scotland
1957	U.S., 8; G.B., 3 one match halved	Minikahda Club, Minneapolis, Minn.
1959	U.S., 9; G.B., 3	Honourable Company of Edinburgh Golfers, Muirfield, Scotland
1961	U.S., 11; G.B., 1	Seattle Golf Club, Seattle, Wash.
1963	U.S., 12; G.B., 8 four matches halved	Ailsa Course, Turnberry, Scotland
1965	G.B., 11; U.S., 11 two matches halved	Baltimore C.C., Five Farms, Baltimore, Md.
1967	U.S., 13; G.B., 7 four matches halved	Royal St George's G.C., Sandwich
1969	U.S., 10; G.B., 8 six matches halved	Milwaukee C.C., Milwaukee, Wis.
1971	G.B., 13; U.S., 11	St Andrews, Scotland
1973	U.S., 14; G.B., 10	Brookline, Mass.
1975	U.S., 15½; G.B. 8½	St Andrews, Scotland
1977		

Note: Matches are generally referred to as being between U.S. and G.B. Actually G.B. should read Great Britain and Ireland.

RYDER CUP MATCH

Year	Score	Venue
1927	U.S., 9½; G.B., 2½	Worcester Country Club, Worcester, Mass.
1929	G.B., 7; U.S., 5	Moortown, Leeds
1931	U.S., 9; G.B., 3	Scioto Country Club, Columbus, Ohio
1933	G.B., 6½; U.S., 5½	Southport and Ainsdale
1935	U.S., 9; G.B., 3	Ridgewood Country Club, Ridgewood, N.J.
1937	U.S., 8; G.B.. 4	Southport and Ainsdale
1939–		
1946	No matches	
1947	U.S., 11; G.B., 1	Portland Golf Club, Portland, Ore.
1949	U.S., 7; G.B., 5	Ganton, Scarborough
1951	U.S., 9½; G.B., 2½	Pinehurst Country Club, Pinehurst, N.C.
1953	U.S., 6½; G.B., 5½	Wentworth, Virginia Water
1955	U.S., 8; G.B., 4	Thunderbird Ranch and Country Club, Palm Springs, Calif.
1957	G.B., 7½; U.S., 4½	Lindrick Golf Club, Notts.
1959	U.S., 8½; G.B., 3½	Eldorado Country Club, Palm Desert, Calif.
1961	U.S., 14½; G.B., 9½	Royal Lytham and St Annes
1963	U.S., 23; G.B., 9	East Lake Country Club, Atlanta, Ga.
1965	U.S., 19½; G.B., 12½	Royal Birkdale
1967	U.S., 23½; G.B., 8½	Champions Golf Club, Houston, Texas
1969	U.S., 16; G.B., 16	Royal Birkdale
1971	U.S., 18½; G.B., 13½	Old Warson Country Club, St Louis, Mo.
1973	U.S., 19; G.B., 13	Muirfield
1975	U.S., 18; G.B., 8	Laurel Valley, Pa.
1977		